Volume **18** **THE**
GOLDEN BOOK
ENCYCLOPEDIA

Taft to Utah

ta-ut

**An exciting, up-to-date encyclopedia
in 20 fact-filled, entertaining volumes**

**Especially designed as
a first encyclopedia for
today's grade-school children**

**More than 2,500 full-color
photographs and illustrations**

GOLDEN®

From the Publishers of Golden® Books

Western Publishing Company, Inc.
Racine, Wisconsin 53404

ILLUSTRATION CREDITS
(t=top, b=bottom, c=center, l=left, r=right)

1 r, Lloyd P. Birmingham; 3 b, © Joe Viesti; 4 bl, Culver Pictures; 4 br, U.S. Army; 5, Bettmann Archive; 6, The Metropolitan Museum of Art, Gift of John D. Rockefeller, Jr., The Cloisters Collection, 1937 (37.80.6); 7, Robert Frank/Melissa Turk & The Artist Network; 8 br, Lloyd P. Birmingham; 9, Historical Pictures Service, Chicago; 10 both, Robert Frank/Melissa Turk & The Artist Network; 11, Bettmann Archive; 12 b, Dennis O'Brien/Joseph, Mindlin & Mulvey Inc.; 13 tl, Courtesy Canon, U.S.A. Inc.; 13 br, Courtesy of AT&T Archives; 14, Tom McHugh/Photo Researchers; 15 tl, Junebug Clark/Photo Researchers; 15 tr, Helen Marcus/Photo Researchers; 15 b, Bonnie Freer/Photo Researchers; 16 tl, Zenith; 16 b, Tom Powers/Joseph, Mindlin & Mulvey Inc.; 17, David Lindroth Inc.; 19 tr, Marilyn Bass; 19 cl, © Joe Viesti; 20 tr, Focus on Sports; 20 b, David Lindroth Inc.; 21, Dennis O'Brien/Joseph, Mindlin & Mulvey Inc.; 23 tc and cr, Marilyn Bass; 23 br, Richard Reynolds/Texas Tourist Development Agency; 24 br, Mathias Oppersdorff/Photo Researchers; 25, Bruce Roberts/Photo Researchers; 26, Richard Hutchings; 27 tr, Culver Pictures; 27 bl and 28 tl, Michael O'Reilly/Joseph, Mindlin & Mulvey Inc.; 28 br, Dennis O'Brien/Joseph, Mindlin & Mulvey Inc.; 29 both, Tourism New Brunswick, Canada; 30 bl, E.R. Degginger/Bruce Coleman Inc.; 30 br and 31, Fiona Reid/Melissa Turk & The Artist Network; 33, Gary Lippincott/Publishers' Graphics; 34 t, Don and Pat Valenti/Taurus Photos; 34 c, Courtesy of Seth Thomas Division, General Time Corporation; 34 b, A. de Menil/Photo Researchers; 35, David E. Edgerton/Photo Researchers; 36, Will McIntyre/Photo Researchers; 37 t, Robert Sischy/Leo de Wys Inc.; 37 br, Lloyd P. Birmingham; 38 b, E.R. Degginger/Bruce Coleman Inc.; 39 tl, Bettmann Archive; 39 br, Robert Frank/Melissa Turk & The Artist Network; 40 tl, Bettmann Archive; 40-41 b, Marcus Hamilton; 41 t, Edward R. Degginger/Bruce Coleman Inc.; 42, Paolo Koch/Photo Researchers; 43, Edna Douthat/Photo Researchers; 44, Robert Frank/Melissa Turk & The Artist Network; 45 t, Marcus Hamilton; 45 inset, Scala/Art Resource; 46 and 47 all, Focus on Sports; 48, Hank Morgan/Science Source/Photo Researchers; 49 tl, Joseph Nettis/Photo Researchers; 49 tr, Tom McHugh/Photo Researchers; 50-51, David Rickman/Publishers' Graphics; 54, Bill Reaves/Viesti Associates; 55, Bettmann Archive; 56-57 t, John Rice/Joseph, Mindlin & Mulvey Inc.; 57 br, Juan Barberis/Melissa Turk & The Artist Network; 58, David Lindroth Inc.; 59, George Holton/Photo Researchers; 60-61, Tom Powers/Joseph, Mindlin & Mulvey Inc.; 62, Harry S. Truman Library; 63, Culver Pictures; 64 bl, Wayne Lankinen/Bruce Coleman Inc.; 64 br, W.E. Ruth/Bruce Coleman Inc.; 64 inset, Nancy Simmerman/Bruce Coleman Inc.; 65, Michelangelo Durazzo/ANA/Viesti Associates; 66, Tom Powers/Joseph, Mindlin & Mulvey Inc.; 68, Robert Frerck/Woodfin Camp; 69 tl, Noble Proctor/Photo Researchers; 69 b, Fiona Reid/Melissa Turk & The Artist Network; 70, Michael Jacobs/Woodfin Camp; 72 bl, Arthur Sirdofsky; 72 cr, Brad Hamann; 72 br, Xerox; 73 br, Bettmann Archive; 74, Michael O'Reilly/Joseph, Mindlin & Mulvey Inc.; 75 tl, Arthur Sirdofksy; 75 tr, Camp Cody for Boys, Freedom, New Hampshire; 77 tr, L.L.T. Rhodes/Taurus Photos; 78 tl, Vandystadt/Photo Researchers; 78 tr, Farrell Grehan/Photo Researchers; 79 tl, Northern Ireland Tourist Board; 79 tr, Susan McCartney/Photo Researchers; 80 tr, George Holton/Photo Researchers; 80 br, Lisl Steiner/Photo Researchers; 81 bl, Uri Golani/UN Photo 152,352; 81 br, John Isaac/UN Photo 151,125; 82-83 all, David Lindroth Inc.; 84 bl, Susan Johns/Photo Researchers; 84 br, Ray Ellis/Photo Researchers; 85, Steve Skloot/Photo Researchers; 87-92, David Rickman/Publishers' Graphics; 93, Virginia Division of Tourism; 94 bl, David Lindroth Inc.; 94 cl, Jet Propulsion Laboratory; 95 tr, Thomas Hoepker/Woodfin Camp; 95 cr, Marilyn Bass; 96, Jose Azel/Contact/Woodfin Camp.

COVER CREDITS
Center: © Joe Viesti. Clockwise from top: Michael Jacobs/Woodfin Camp; Fiona Reid/Melissa Turk & The Artist Network; Helen Marcus/Photo Researchers; © Western Publishing Company, Inc.; © Western Publishing Company, Inc.; Tom McHugh/Photo Researchers.

Library of Congress Catalog Card Number: 87-82741
ISBN: 0-307-70118-2

ABCDEFGHIJK

The letter *T* was first written by the ancient Egyptians as a simple check mark.

The ancient Semites had a letter they called *taw*. This was their word for "mark."

Both the ancient Greeks and Romans moved the bar to the top.

Taft, William H., *see* **presidents of the U.S.**

Taiwan, *see* **China**

Taj Mahal

The Taj Mahal, in northern India, is one of the world's most beautiful buildings. It was built in the 1600s as a *tomb*—burial place—for Mumtaz Mahal, the wife of the Indian ruler Shah Jahan. The building was named in her honor.

Mumtaz Mahal died in 1631 while giving birth to her 14th child. Shah Jahan began construction of the Taj Mahal the following year. It took 22 years and about 20,000 workers to complete the tomb, walkways, towers, and gardens that make up the Taj Mahal.

The tomb is built of white marble and sits on a platform of sandstone. Colorful stones decorate its walls. Quotations from the Koran—the Moslem holy book—are carved into the outside walls. The building is topped by a huge dome. There are four high *minarets* —prayer towers—one at each corner of the platform. Pools in the garden outside reflect the building's beauty.

Shah Jahan and his wife are buried in an underground room under the main building.

See also **architecture.**

The Taj Mahal is one of the world's most beautiful buildings. It was built in India in the 1600s by Shah Jahan as a tomb for his wife Mumtaz Mahal.

tall tale

A tall tale is a wildly unbelievable story. Tall tales are often about real or imaginary folk heroes. They are usually very funny and full of exaggerations and impossible events.

Tall tales started out as spoken stories. The more popular ones were later written down and printed in newspapers and magazines. Many were written in *dialect* to keep the feeling of a spoken story. A dialect is the way people in a particular area talk.

Telling and listening to tall tales have long been enjoyable pastimes. After a hard day of cutting down trees, lumberjacks have often entertained each other with stories about Paul Bunyan. Bunyan was a giant lumberjack. According to one story, he tamed a blizzard by tying it down. Cowboys often told of Pecos Bill, the super-cowboy who roped a tornado and rode it to Arizona. (*See* **Bunyan, Paul** and **Pecos Bill.**)

John Henry was a black folk hero. Stories and songs told of his great strength as a "steel-driving man" on the railroad. The most famous story, about how John Henry pits his strength against a machine and wins, may have been based on a real event. (*See* **Henry, John.**)

Davy Crockett and Mike Fink were real men whose adventures and skills became the subjects of tall tales. Davy Crockett was born in Tennessee in 1786. He became a famous frontiersman. Later, he served in Congress, and he died fighting for Texan independence at the Alamo in 1836. But it is unlikely that he once tamed a bear and taught him to whistle and churn butter, as one tale claims. (*See* **Crockett, Davy.**)

Mike Fink operated a *keelboat* on the Ohio and Mississippi rivers. Keelboats had flat bottoms and were designed to pull heavy loads through shallow water. During Fink's lifetime—from around 1770 to 1823—his bragging and his shooting skill gave rise to many tall tales. According to these tales, Fink enjoyed playing jokes, sometimes cruel ones. One story is about a shooting match Fink had with a man named Carpenter. They each aimed at a tin cup on the other's head. One of Carpenter's shots accidentally scratched Fink. Fink became angry. He shot Carpenter in the head, killing him. One of Carpenter's friends then shot and killed Mike Fink.

See also **myths and legends.**

tank

A tank is a large armored vehicle that travels like a tractor on *caterpillar treads*—wide metal belts. A gun that can swivel around is mounted on the outside, and soldiers ride inside.

Left, a tank from World War I travels over rough ground. Right, a modern M-1 Abrams tank of the U.S. Army has powerful guns and a rocket launcher.

During World War I (1914 to 1917), both France and Britain were looking for a solution to the same problem. They needed to find a way to move their armies across large areas filled with enemy trenches. A four-wheeled vehicle would fall into the trenches. But a vehicle using caterpillar treads instead of wheels could drive over the trenches. Ernest D. Swinton, a British colonel, is given credit for inventing the tank. At just about the same time, a Frenchman, Colonel Jean B. Estienne, also developed a tank.

Tanks were first used in combat in the Battle of the Somme, in France in 1916. The tanks gained some ground, but many of them broke down or got stuck in the mud. A year later, the tanks were more successful. By the end of the war, France and Britain were building and using tanks. Germany used tanks captured from the French and British. The United States built tanks, but these were not used in battle.

Tanks were very important during World War II (1939 to 1945). They carried machine guns, rockets, or flamethrowers. Some tanks were *amphibious*—they could cross rivers as well as travel on land.

Tanks are still being used today, but the invention of new antitank weapons have made them less effective.

See also **weapon.**

Tanzania, *see* Africa

tap dance

Tap dance is a dance style in which dancers tap out exciting rhythms with their shoes. Tap shoes have small metal plates—*taps*—on their heels and toes, so the sound of the movements can be heard clearly.

Tap dancing began in the United States. It grew out of two sources. The owners of black slaves would not let the slaves beat on drums. So the slaves danced traditional African dances, and made dance rhythms by clapping and by stamping their feet. During

Bill ("Bojangles") Robinson, one of the great stars of tap dance.

the same time period, Irish and Scottish dancers sometimes danced in wooden shoes called *clogs*. The heavy shoes clumped and brushed to the dance rhythms.

Sometime in the 1800s, these two kinds of dancing came together. Dancers—both black and white—attached noisemakers to the bottoms of their shoes. Music halls set up dance contests and let the audience decide who was best.

Tap dancing was most popular between 1910 and 1940. Famous tap stars like Bill ("Bojangles") Robinson toured the cities. In the 1930s, tap dancers were featured in movie musicals. Some of the most famous tap routines were performed by Fred Astaire and Gene Kelly. Their movies play often on television.

See also **dance.**

tape recording, *see* sound recording

tapestry

A tapestry is a piece of woven art. Skilled weavers work colored yarns into shapes and patterns, and into scenes of people and animals. The finished tapestry is usually hung on a wall.

A tapestry is woven on a frame called a *loom.* Plain yarn is stretched between the loom's upper and lower beams. These yarns make up the *warp.* Colored yarns are woven from side to side. These yarns are the *weft.* They may pass over and under the warp yarns or be wrapped around each warp yarn. The design is created by changing the color of the weft yarns. The weaver follows a drawing called a *cartoon* that shows the pattern and colors of the tapestry. The weft yarns are pushed close together, so you see only the colorful design and none of the warp.

A detail from *The Hunt of the Unicorn,* a group of tapestries woven around 1500.

People have been weaving tapestries for thousands of years. The oldest examples we have were made in Egypt around 1400 B.C. During the Middle Ages in Europe—A.D. 500 to 1500—tapestries hung on the walls of churches and castles. These large tapestries showed scenes from the Bible, history, and daily life. Beautiful tapestries of animals and patterns have been woven in Peru for hundreds of years.

tar

Tar is a thick, black, sticky liquid that dries to form a slightly rubbery solid. People have used tar for centuries to fill cracks in roofs and ships. Tar is so closely associated with ships that sailors are nicknamed "tars."

Tar can be made from wood or coal. At the start of the 1900s, most of the chemicals used to make dyes, drugs, and plastics were produced by heating coal inside airless furnaces. When the fumes were cooled, they separated into water and a thick black liquid called *coal tar.* Coal tar is the source of hundreds of chemicals. The desired chemicals are removed, and tar is left behind.

The process of making tar from wood is similar. As wood is heated in an airless oven, some chemicals gradually boil off. At first, the wood becomes charcoal. If the heating continues, the wood breaks down into tar. But most tar comes from coal, since the chemicals from coal tar are valuable, and wood is better used in other ways.

Asphalt—sometimes called *pitch*—is a natural material similar to tar and is used for many of the same purposes. Artificial asphalt is material left when petroleum oil is heated. (*See* **asphalt.**)

taste

The sense of taste is stimulated when food touches the taste buds on your tongue.

Your tongue is covered with small bumps. On some parts of the tongue, these bumps are small and hard to see. Toward the back

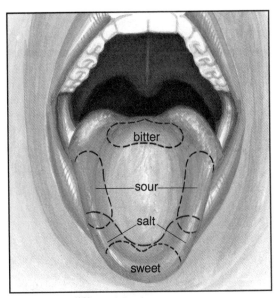

bitter

sour

salt

sweet

We detect different tastes on different areas of the tongue.

of the tongue, they are larger. The taste buds surround each bump. They are the organs of taste.

When you eat, your salivary glands produce saliva. The saliva mixes with the food, and your taste buds become bathed in the food-and-saliva mixture. Substances in the food stimulate your taste buds. Messages about the tastes are sent by nerves to the brain.

All animals seem to have a sense of taste. Some fish have taste organs in the skin. Some insects can sense taste through organs on their hairy legs or their antennae.

Humans respond to four tastes—sweet, bitter, sour, and salty. The taste buds for sweetness are on the tip of the tongue. The taste buds for bitterness are at the back of the tongue. Sourness is tasted along the sides of the tongue. Salt is tasted at the tip of the tongue and along the sides.

To find the location of the different taste buds, you can do a simple experiment. Mix a tablespoon of each of the four tastes. Saltwater, sugar water, water mixed with vinegar, and unsweetened grapefruit juice work well. Use a separate toothpick for each flavor. Dip the toothpick into the vinegar water and touch it to various spots on your tongue.

Draw a map of your tongue and mark where you taste sourness. Do the same with the other liquids.

What we usually call the sense of taste is actually the senses of taste and smell working together. While you are chewing, the smell of the food drifts up the back of your mouth into your nose. The combination of taste and smell produces a wide variety of delicious flavors. When you have a cold, food loses much of its flavor, because your nose is stuffed up and you cannot smell.

See also **smell.**

tax

A tax is money that people pay to support their government. Tax money pays for the military, highways, public school systems, police protection, health care for the poor and elderly, and many other services. In the United States, people pay taxes to the federal government and to the governments of their states and local communities.

Taxes paid directly to a government by individuals are called *direct taxes. Indirect taxes* are paid to the government by businesses and manufacturers. They get the money to pay these taxes by charging more for their products. For example, cigarette makers pay a tax on tobacco to the federal government. The cost of tobacco products includes the amount of the tax.

The federal government, most state governments, and a few local governments collect a *personal income tax.* This is a tax on the money a person has earned or received from other sources for one year. Businesses pay income taxes based on their profits for the year. Many states also add a *sales tax* to items bought within the state.

Towns and cities raise money by collecting *property tax.* It is paid every year by people who own a building or land.

Taylor, Zachary, *see* **presidents of the U.S.**

The Russian composer Tchaikovsky is famous for his ballet and symphonic music.

Tchaikovsky, Peter Ilich

Peter Ilich Tchaikovsky (chy-KOF-skee) was a famous Russian composer of the late 1800s. His works are still performed all over the world.

Tchaikovsky was born in 1840 and died in 1893. As a young man, he studied law in the Russian city of St. Petersburg (now Leningrad). But he gave up his law studies to study music.

Tchaikovsky studied the music of Beethoven and other great composers of Europe. He also studied the music of his own country. Soon he was writing music that became very popular both in Russia and in Europe.

A ballet company in St. Petersburg asked Tchaikovsky to write music for ballet. His *Swan Lake, Sleeping Beauty,* and *The Nutcracker* are three of the best-loved dance pieces in the world. *The Nutcracker* tells the story of a Christmas gift—a nutcracker—that comes to life.

Tchaikovsky also wrote many pieces for orchestra. One of the most famous is the *1812 Overture.* It celebrates a great Russian victory over an invading French army in the year 1812. In addition to orchestra instruments, this piece calls for cannon and fireworks to imitate the battle. It is often performed at outdoor concerts.

See also **composers.**

tea

Tea is a drink made by putting the dried leaves of the tea plant into boiling-hot water. India and China are the world's leading tea-growing countries.

Tea plants thrive in hot climates with good rainfall. The best tea grows on hills 3,000 to 7,000 feet (910 to 2,100 meters) above sea level. Tea plants are started indoors from seeds. When the plants are about 8 inches (20 centimeters) tall, they are replanted in fields. In about three years, they have grown into bushes about 4 feet (120 centimeters) high and are producing leaves good for tea.

The leaves at the tips are best. After they are picked, tea leaves are *withered*—dried —and rolled. Some leaves are then *fermented.* This is done by placing them in damp, warm rooms. The fermented leaves change to an orange or copper color. Then the tea is *fired*—heated.

There are three types of tea. *Black tea* is fermented. *Green tea* is not. *Oolong tea* is partly fermented. Many teas are blends of different leaves.

Tea is served hot or cold. Like coffee, it contains *caffeine*—a substance that can keep

Blossoms on a tea bush. The dried and treated leaves make the drink called tea.

people awake. Many drinks brewed from hot water, flowers, fruits, spices, and herbs are called "teas," even though they contain no tea leaves.

Tecumseh

Tecumseh (te-KUM-suh) was a Shawnee Indian leader who tried to unite American Indian tribes against the white people who wanted to settle on Indian land.

Tecumseh was born sometime around 1768, near the Mad River in Ohio. After the Revolutionary War, pioneers began to cross the Appalachian Mountains and settle on Indian lands. When Tecumseh was a boy, his father was killed by white men. Tecumseh began to hate the settlers who year after year moved onto more Indian land. As a young man, he fought the settlers. But he soon realized that a much greater effort would be needed to stop them.

Tecumseh worked out a plan with his brother, a Shawnee religious leader called the "Prophet." They decided that the Indian tribes from the Great Lakes to Florida and from the Atlantic Ocean to the Great Plains should unite to defend their land. Tecumseh believed that no one chief had the right to make treaties with the settlers.

To help bring about this plan, Tecumseh traveled among the Indian tribes. He was a convincing speaker, and many tribes promised to join the fight against the settlers. In 1811, while Tecumseh was speaking to tribes in the South, he learned that his brother was dead. During the Battle of Tippecanoe, in Indiana, U.S. forces led by William Henry Harrison had killed the Prophet and his followers.

The Prophet's death made Tecumseh even more determined to fight. During the War of 1812, he joined the British forces, hoping to defeat the Americans. The British were eager to have the Indians help them. They gave the Indians guns and other supplies. They also made Tecumseh a British general in command of all Indian forces.

Tecumseh tried to unite Indian tribes against American settlers.

In 1813, Tecumseh led his men against the Americans at the Battle of the Thames in Ontario, Canada. The U.S. soldiers were led by William Henry Harrison, who later became the ninth president of the United States. Tecumseh fought bravely but was killed during the fighting. After his death, unity among the Indian tribes broke down. The Indians were left with little hope of stopping American settlement on the lands between the Appalachians and the Mississippi River.

See also **War of 1812** and **Indian Wars.**

teeth

Teeth are bonelike structures that are set in the jaws. Teeth are used for chewing, tearing, and biting food. People also use their teeth when they speak because teeth help people make certain sounds. For example, you cannot easily make the *th* sound without placing your tongue against the front teeth. You must put your top and bottom teeth together to make the *s* sound.

Each tooth consists of a *crown* and *roots.* The crown is the part above the gum. The roots are the parts below the gum. Teeth are made of tough tissue called *dentin.* The dentin in the crown is covered with *enamel.* Enamel is the hardest substance in the body. It protects the tooth against decay and the wear and tear of chewing. Inside the dentin is a space filled with *pulp.* Pulp is a softer tissue that contains blood vessels and nerves. The pulp continues into the *root canals*—channels inside the roots. At the bottom of each root, there is an opening through which blood vessels and nerves can enter the tooth.

Human babies are born without teeth. Baby teeth begin to emerge when the child is about six months old. More teeth appear every few weeks. A child usually has a complete set of 20 baby teeth by age 2. These small teeth later fall out, usually when the child is between the ages of 6 and 13. The baby teeth are pushed out and replaced by larger, permanent teeth.

Adult humans have 32 permanent teeth. There are 8 *incisors* at the front of the mouth—4 on the top and 4 on the bottom. The incisors are for biting and cutting. Just behind the incisors are the 4 *canines*—1 on each side, top and bottom. In humans, the canines are used for biting. In many other animals, the sharp canines are used for stabbing and tearing their prey.

The teeth at the back of the jaws are the *premolars* and the *molars.* They are used for grinding and crushing food. There are 8 premolars and 8 molars. A third set of molars—the 4 *wisdom teeth*—usually do not appear until after 18 years of age. Sometimes, the jaw is not large enough for the wisdom teeth. They may cause pain and have to be removed.

Bacteria that are normally in the mouth can form a thin film called *plaque* on the teeth. If not removed, plaque can cause problems. Bacteria in plaque digest sugar on the teeth and produce acids. The acids eat through the enamel layer, causing cavities. Hardened plaque can irritate the gums and cause gum disease. It is important for good health and appearance to keep your teeth clean by brushing and flossing. It is also important to visit a dentist regularly.

See also **dentistry**.

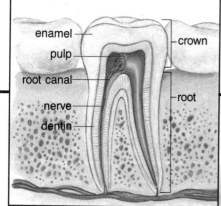

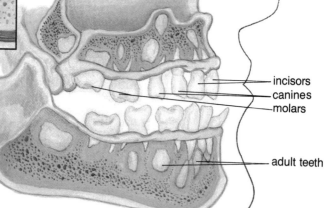

Above, parts of a tooth. Right, an x-ray view of a child's jaw, with the baby teeth still in place. Already, adult teeth are growing under the gums and pushing the baby teeth out.

In the 1800s, a telegrapher could send messages in Morse code at 50 words per minute. In Morse code, different combinations of dots and dashes stand for different letters.

telegraph

On May 24, 1844, Samuel Morse demonstrated an invention that changed the way we send messages. Until then, messages traveled by foot, horse, or boat. It could take a message hours, weeks, or months to arrive. But Morse sent a message from Baltimore, Maryland, to Washington, D.C.—a distance of 64 kilometers (40 miles)—in just seconds. His invention was the telegraph. (*See* **Morse, Samuel F. B.**)

The telegraph uses electricity to send messages over wires. The messages are sent in a code called the *Morse code.* This code uses a pattern of dots and dashes to stand for letters in the alphabet and for punctuation. The telegraph operator forms the dots and dashes by pressing the *sending key*—a switch in the electrical curcuit. When the sending key is pressed, the circuit is complete and the electricity flows. When it is released, the circuit is broken and the flow stops. Quickly releasing the sending key forms a dot. Holding it down a moment forms a dash.

The wire that carries the electrical signal connects the sender to the receiver. The receiver has an electromagnet and an iron strip. When the electricity is flowing, the electromagnet attracts the iron strip. This makes a clicking sound. A dot pulls the iron strip and electromagnet together for an instant. A dash pulls them together for a bit longer. To decode the message, the person receiving the message listens to the pattern of clicks.

Morse's telegraph has since been improved. By 1872, two messages could be sent over the same wire at the same time. Two years later, Edison improved this so four messages could be sent. (*See* **Edison, Thomas Alva.**)

The *Teletype* machine made it possible for messages to be sent and received as words instead of in Morse code. Teletype machines are used in news offices, stock exchanges, and many other businesses. The Teletype operator types the message on a keyboard resembling a typewriter. The machine punches holes in a paper tape. The tape passes through an automatic *transmitter* —sender. It sends the message in Morse code to another Teletype machine. This machine then prints the message as words.

Today's Teletype machines send hundreds of words per minute—and other information, too. It is now common to send photographs by telegraph. Even if you have never received a personal telegraph, you can find pictures and stories in almost any newspaper that were sent and received by telegraph.

telephone

In 1876, Alexander Graham Bell patented a new way to communicate—the telephone. The word *telephone* means "to speak from a distance." But the telephone does more. It lets people at either end speak and listen, ask questions or answer them, without any delay. Messages are carried just as they are sent, so that you can recognize the voice as well as hear the words.

How It Works When you speak into a telephone's *transmitter*—mouthpiece—the sound waves from your voice are changed into electrical signals. These are carried to the *receiver*—earpiece—of the telephone at the other end. The receiver changes the electrical signals back to sound waves. When a telephone call is in progress, the transmitters and receivers of both telephones are working at the same time.

The transmitter is made of two main parts—a *carbon chamber* and a *diaphragm.* The carbon chamber contains particles of the element carbon. When the carbon particles touch each other, they conduct electricity. The diaphragm is a thin, flexible metal disk that fits over the carbon chamber. When you speak, your voice creates sound waves that press against the diaphragm. As the diaphragm is pressed, it packs the carbon particles in the chamber more tightly together. This increases the electric current.

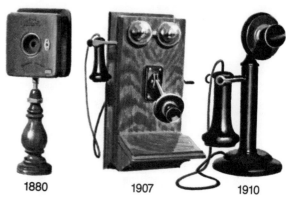

1880   1907   1910
Early telephones had no dials or buttons. An operator connected calls for you.

The louder you speak, the stronger the sound waves, and the stronger the electrical transmission. When you lower your voice or stop speaking, pressure on the diaphragm eases and the electric current decreases.

The telephone receiver has a diaphragm, too. The receiver diaphragm is placed over an *electromagnet,* such as a piece of iron with a wire coil around it. When current runs through the electromagnet, it becomes magnetized and pulls the diaphragm in, toward it. A strong current pulls harder than a weak one. The changes in current make the diaphragm *vibrate*—move rapidly back and forth. These vibrations reach your ear as sound waves.

The body of the telephone contains an *amplifier.* This increases the strength of the electrical signals that are transmitted and received. The telephone body also contains a switching device that lets you "connect" with another telephone. Another important

TELEPHONE TRANSMISSION

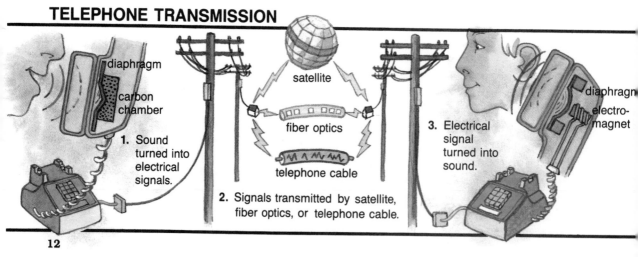

diaphragm
carbon chamber
1. Sound turned into electrical signals.

satellite
fiber optics
telephone cable
2. Signals transmitted by satellite, fiber optics, or telephone cable.

3. Electrical signal turned into sound.
diaphragm
electro-magnet

A "fax" machine can receive a letter or even a picture over normal telephone lines.

feature is a signal—a sound or light—to let you know when someone is calling.

Making Connections In the early days of the telephone, calls were placed by an *operator,* a person who connected the lines on a switchboard. As more people got telephones, automatic switching equipment was developed to do much of this work.

When you dial or push the buttons of a telephone to call someone, you are sending out a set of numbers—the area code, the local exchange, and the last, four-digit number. These numbers are a set of instructions from the switching device in your telephone to the switching mechanisms in a central telephone office. With today's telephone systems, you can call many of the world's cities just by using sets of code numbers.

As telephone systems began using computers, push-button telephones began replacing the older rotary-dial phones. When a number is dialed with a rotary dial, the switching system in the telephone must count the number of clicks as the dial returns to its resting position. Push-button phones produce a single tone for each button pressed. This sends a faster, clearer signal to the computers that help place the call.

Push-button phones do much more than shorten the time needed to make a connection. They also allow a caller to connect with a computer by pressing buttons to produce a code. In some computerized telephone systems, callers can use code numbers to connect to recorded messages.

Advances in Telephoning The *radiotelephone* was invented in 1900. It is still in use today on ships and aircraft, and in some private cars. Telephone signals are sent without wires, as radio signals. The radio signals are received and are changed back to a normal telephone current. This current is then changed into sound waves. Recently, large cities have installed *cellular* telephone systems. A cellular system enables many radiotelephone users to make and receive calls at the same time.

The first transatlantic telephone cable was laid in 1956. This cable connected callers in Europe and the Americas. Today, new *fiber-optic* cables are being used, on land and under the sea, to carry more messages at the same time than ever before. Fiber-optic cables have no metal wire. They carry telephone signals in the form of a thin beam of pulsing light.

The telephone is still used to speak from a distance. Modern technology has made it possible to beam telephone signals from satellites many miles above the earth. Today, we also send copies of printed text or pictures by telephone, and do our banking by telephone.

See also **Bell, Alexander Graham.**

This novelty telephone looks like a cartoon character.

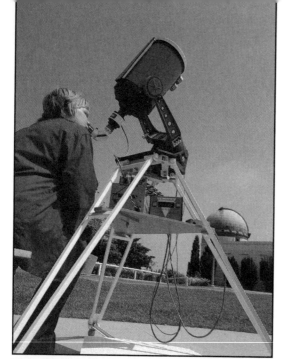

This young astronomer is observing the sun through a solar telescope.

telescope

A telescope is a device used to *magnify*—enlarge—the image of a distant object. It is an important tool for astronomers. It enables them to see much farther into space than is possible with the unaided eye.

Telescopes that take in light are called *optical telescopes*. The light enters one end and is focused by one or more glass lenses or mirrors. The light leaves through a small lens called the *eyepiece* and you see the enlarged image. Other kinds of telescopes magnify other kinds of energy, such as X rays and infrared radiation. *Radio telescopes* take in radio waves.

The first telescope was invented around 1600. It had a long, hollow tube with a glass lens at each end. This kind of telescope is called a *refracting* telescope because the lenses *refract*—bend—the light as it passes through them. Small telescopes, such as a sailor's spyglass or an opera glass, work this way.

In 1668, Sir Isaac Newton built the first of another kind of telescope—a *reflecting* telescope. A reflecting telescope has a curved mirror that reflects and focuses the light. (*See* **Newton, Sir Isaac.**)

Very big telescopes used by astronomers are usually reflecting telescopes. An astronomer can look at the image through an eyepiece, photograph it, or analyze it with special electronic equipment.

The giant Hale telescope at Mount Palomar in California was completed in 1948. For many years, it was the world's largest and most effective telescope. Its light-collecting mirror is 200 inches (about 5 meters) across. The size of the mirror is important. The bigger the mirror, the more light the telescope can collect. That can mean the difference between seeing a very faint object through the telescope and seeing nothing at all. In 1974, a telescope with a 236-inch (6-meter) mirror was completed in the Soviet Union. Various larger telescopes are now being planned and will soon be the leaders in astronomy.

See also **lens; observatory;** and **radio telescope.**

television

Television is a way to send pictures and sound electronically. In the United States and many other countries, nearly every household has at least one television set. Television provides people with many kinds of entertainment, including comedy shows, dramas, movies, and sports. It also provides important news and information.

History of Television In the late 1800s, many inventors were trying to find ways to use electricity to send signals. At first, they were able to send codes by radio waves. Then they learned how to send voice messages through the air. In the 1920s, people bought radios for their homes, and radio stations began *broadcasting*—sending out—news, music, and entertainment.

In 1923, Vladimir Zworykin, a Russian-born inventor, made a television camera tube. He improved the camera tube and named it the *iconoscope*. It was an important step toward picking up an image and turning it into an electric signal. The first moving television images were broadcast in 1926 by John Logie Baird, a Scotsman. A year later, Philo Farnsworth, an American inventor, patented an improved *orthicon* tube. This device changes light images into electronic signals so they can be transmitted.

Early television receivers were large and expensive and only a few homes had one. Starting in the late 1940s, smaller and less expensive receivers became available. These television sets could show only black-and-white pictures. By the middle of the

Television camera operators (above left) may send live reports to their station or record events for broadcast later. Below, news reporters appear live in the studio. In a control room (above right), live and recorded scenes are selected for broadcast.

This 1951 television needed a bulky cabinet to fit the receiver. Today, a television can be about the size of a large wristwatch.

1950s, most homes in the United States had a television set.

The first television stations were begun by radio broadcasters. These stations broadcast old movies and shows performed live before the television camera. There was no easy way to record a show for later broadcast.

In 1953, television broadcasters agreed on a method of sending color images. People began buying color receivers.

By the end of the 1950s, television stations were using video-recording equipment to record programs. One use of video recorders is to play back what has been recorded, such as an exciting football or baseball play. This "instant replay" helped make television sports very popular. Recording equipment was very large and expensive. Only broadcasters could afford it.

Video recorders for home use became popular in the 1980s. With recorders connected to their television sets, people can record a show, and then watch it whenever they wish. They can also buy or rent videotapes of movies and play them on their television sets. (*See* **video recording.**)

How Television Works A television camera changes light images into electronic signals. These signals can either be sent out immediately, or they can be recorded on videotape for later broadcast. The sound for the television program is changed into electronic signals, too.

Television signals are usually *transmitted* —sent—through the air from an antenna on a hill or tall building. The signals from most American stations can be received within about 50 miles (80 kilometers) in any direction from the *transmitter*. Reception is best at night when the weather is clear and dry.

HOW A TV SET MAKES A PICTURE

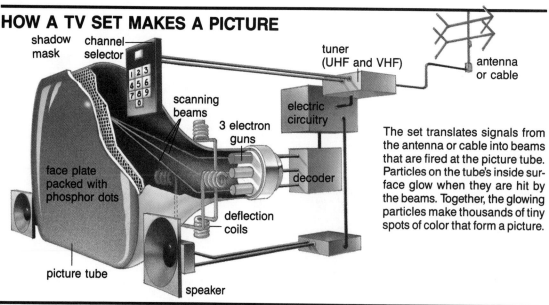

shadow mask
channel selector
tuner (UHF and VHF)
antenna or cable
scanning beams
3 electron guns
electric circuitry
face plate packed with phosphor dots
decoder
deflection coils
picture tube
speaker

The set translates signals from the antenna or cable into beams that are fired at the picture tube. Particles on the tube's inside surface glow when they are hit by the beams. Together, the glowing particles make thousands of tiny spots of color that form a picture.

Television signals may also be transmitted through a *cable*. Signals received by cable are not affected by weather, surrounding buildings, or by interference.

The programs sent by a television station are picked up with a *receiver*—a television set. The television set's *tuner*—channel selector—lets you select one of many signals from the air or the cable. The receiver changes electronic signals back into pictures and sound.

The picture signals are turned into an electric current by an *electron gun* at the back of the television picture tube. This gun shoots a beam of *electrons*—tiny particles with an electrical charge—at the inner surface of the picture tube. This surface is coated with a layer of *phosphors*—materials that glow when hit by electrons. In a color television set, there are phosphors that glow blue, green, and red.

The beam of electrons shot from the gun crosses the picture tube 525 times to form a single image. It forms 30 images each second! We watch the outside of the picture tube—the screen. The images change so quickly that they appear to be moving.

Meanwhile, the sound signal is carried to an *amplifier* in the receiver. The amplifier changes the sound signals into electricity that powers a speaker in the television set. (*See* **amplifier.**)

Long-Distance Television In 1965, the communications satellite *Early Bird* was launched. Television broadcasters could bounce signals off the satellite to a distant part of the world. Today, television signals can be sent from almost any point on Earth to any other point by way of a communications satellite. Sports events such as the Olympic Games can be broadcast live everywhere. (*See* **communications satellite.**)

People who live far from local television stations sometimes have a receiver called a *satellite dish*. Such a dish receives television signals directly from satellites. They may be able to receive programs broadcast thousands of miles away!

temperature scale

A temperature scale provides a way of measuring how hot or cold something is. Temperature is usually measured with an instrument called a *thermometer*. (*See* **thermometer; heat;** and **cold.**)

Two temperature scales are commonly used—the *Fahrenheit scale* and the *Celsius scale*. The Celsius scale used to be called the *centigrade scale*. The freezing point of water—the point at which it forms ice—is 0° C (0 degrees Celsius) or 32° F (32 degrees Fahrenheit). The boiling point of water—the temperature at which it turns to steam—is 100° C or 212° F. So there are 100 Celsius degrees but 180 Fahrenheit degrees between the freezing point of water and its boiling point. This means that a Celsius degree represents almost twice the temperature difference of a Fahrenheit degree.

Many scientists need to use a third temperature scale, called the *Kelvin scale*. The Kelvin scale starts at the coldest possible temperature, which is called *absolute zero*. Absolute zero is −273° C (−460° F). The Kelvin degree unit is the same size as the Celsius degree unit.

See also **measurement.**

TWO TEMPERATURE SCALES

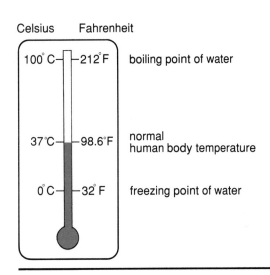

Celsius   Fahrenheit

100° C — 212° F   boiling point of water

37°C — 98.6°F   normal
human body temperature

0°C — 32° F   freezing point of water

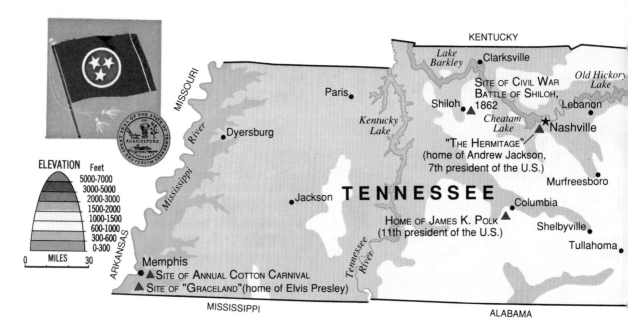

ELEVATION Feet
5000-7000
3000-5000
2000-3000
1500-2000
1000-1500
600-1000
300-600
0-300

0 MILES 30

Tennessee

Capital: Nashville
Area: 42,144 square miles (109,153 square kilometers) (34th-largest state)
Population (1980): 4,591,120 (1985): about 4,762,000 (17th-largest state)
Became a state: June 1, 1796 (16th state)

Tennessee is a state in the east-central United States. It is world-famous for its music. The city of Nashville is the center of the country-and-western recording industry.

Tennessee is bordered on the north by Kentucky and Virginia. North Carolina is to the east, and Georgia, Alabama, and Mississippi are to the south. Arkansas and Missouri are on the west.

Land Tennessee has a mild climate and receives a good amount of rainfall. The eastern part of the state is in the Blue Ridge and Appalachian mountains. The highest point in the state is Clingmans Dome. It rises 6,643 feet (2,025 meters) above sea level. The mountains are rich in coal, zinc, copper, and limestone, and mining is the chief economic activity in this region.

Central Tennessee is rolling farmland. Farmers raise dairy and beef cattle, hogs, and sheep. Western Tennessee is a lowland area where cotton is the chief crop. This area is also the home of the famous Tennessee walking horse—a horse developed especially to work on plantations.

The Tennessee River loops through the state. Dams built by the Tennessee Valley Authority (TVA) have made it the best-controlled river in the world. The dams provide electricity and help prevent floods. They have also created 28 reservoirs, which are sometimes called the "Great Lakes of the South." They form a waterway that stretches from eastern Tennessee to the Ohio River. The reservoirs are popular vacation spots for fishermen and boaters.

History About 1,000 years ago, Indians called Mound Builders lived in Tennessee. Their name comes from their custom of burying their dead in large mounds of earth. European explorers visited the area in the middle 1500s and saw villages of Cherokee, Chickasaw, and Creek Indians. Trappers and traders worked in the region. But there were no permanent European settlements until 1769, when settlers from North Carolina and Virginia moved into Tennessee. In 1784, the independent state of Franklin was formed in eastern Tennessee. It lasted for four years. By 1796, Tennessee had enough people to become a state.

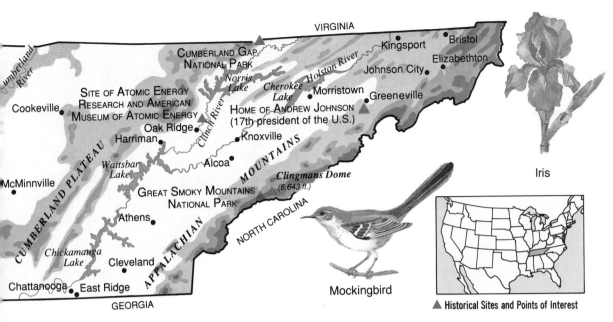

VIRGINIA

Cumberland River

CUMBERLAND GAP NATIONAL PARK

Kingsport • Bristol
Johnson City • Elizabethton
• Greeneville
Morristown

Norris Lake
Cherokee Lake
Holston River

SITE OF ATOMIC ENERGY RESEARCH AND AMERICAN MUSEUM OF ATOMIC ENERGY
HOME OF ANDREW JOHNSON (17th president of the U.S.)

Cookeville •

Oak Ridge
Harriman •
Clinch River
Knoxville
Alcoa •

McMinnville •

Wattsbar Lake

GREAT SMOKY MOUNTAINS NATIONAL PARK

Clingmans Dome (6,643 ft.)

Athens •

APPALACHIAN MOUNTAINS

NORTH CAROLINA

CUMBERLAND PLATEAU

Chickamauga Lake
Cleveland •

Chattanooga • East Ridge

GEORGIA

Iris

Mockingbird

▲ Historical Sites and Points of Interest

A country music festival in Smithville. Tennessee is the home of country music.

The Indians and the settlers fought for control of the land. Andrew Jackson—who later became the 7th president of the United States—played an important role in defeating the Creek Indians. The Chicasaw sold their land to the government in 1818. In 1838, the Cherokee were driven out of Tennessee. The state gradually changed from a rugged frontier—where independent frontiersmen such as Davy Crockett lived—into an agricultural state. (*See* **Jackson, Andrew** and **Crockett, Davy.**)

Tennessee was also the home of James K. Polk, the 11th U.S. president. While Polk was president, his home state sent so many soldiers to fight in the Mexican War that Tennessee became known as the "Volunteer State." (*See* **Mexican War.**)

Before and during the Civil War (1861 to 1865), Tennessee was badly split over whether to *secede*—separate from the Union. In 1861, it did secede and joined the Confederate States of America. Nevertheless, many men from Tennessee fought on the side of the North. (*See* **Civil War.**)

People Tennessee today is one of the nation's major tobacco-producing states. Livestock, dairy products, wheat, corn, and cotton are also important to the state's economy. Chemicals, textiles, clothes, electrical machinery, and furniture are among Tennessee's manufactured items. No other state produces more hardwood flooring, marble, zinc, and the mineral pyrite.

More than half of the state's people live in cities. Memphis, the largest city, is on the Mississippi River. It is an important port and a center for the manufacture and trade of cotton and lumber products.

Nashville is the capital and second-largest city, located in the middle of the state. Besides being famous as the country music capital of the world, it is a commercial, industrial, and transportation center.

One of Tennessee's newest cities is Oak Ridge, in the eastern part of the state. Oak Ridge was built secretly during World War II as a place for producing uranium, an element needed for atomic bombs. Today, it is a center for research into peaceful uses of nuclear energy.

tennis

tennis

Tennis is a sport played by millions of people around the world. Games are played indoors and outdoors by two or four people. In the United States, tennis courts are found in many public parks and schools.

A *singles match* is a game of tennis played by two people. A *doubles match* is played by four people. Players use tennis rackets to hit a ball back and forth over a net. The object of the game is to hit the ball so that the opponent cannot return it. Players must have strength, skill, and quickness.

The court is a flat, rectangular area of grass, concrete, or clay. Singles matches are played on courts that are 78 feet (23.4 meters) long and 27 feet (8.1 meters) wide. For doubles matches, the court is 9 feet (2.7 meters) wider. A net 3½ feet (107 centimeters) high stretches across the middle of the court. Players face one another on opposite sides of the net.

A tennis ball is hollow and slightly smaller than a baseball. The outside is covered with a soft, fuzzy material. Most tennis rackets are about 27 inches (68 centimeters) long. The racket's frame is made of wood or lightweight metal. The oval face of the racket is a

A champion tennis player can serve the ball at nearly 100 miles per hour!

web of tight strings. Leather wound around the handle gives the player a good grip.

Players score by winning points, games, sets, and matches. To win a game, a player must score four points and be at least two

The server stands behind the back line on one side of the center mark and hits the ball into the service area on the opposite side of the court.

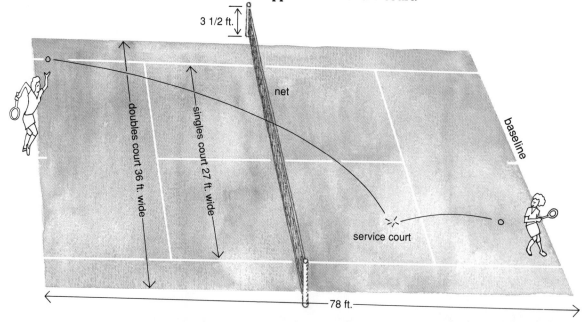

points ahead of his or her opponent. The first player to win six games wins a *set.* To win a tennis *match,* a player usually has to win two sets. Sometimes, a player must win three out of five sets to win the match. There are special scoring rules if a game or set is tied.

To begin the game, a player *serves* the ball—tosses it into the air and swings the racket at it. This should send the ball over the net to the other side of the court. If the ball hits the net or lands outside the court, the player has committed a *fault.* All play stops. The player has a second chance. If the second serve is bad, the player has made a *double fault* and loses a point.

Once a ball has been served, the opposing player must return it before it hits the ground twice. Hitting a ball while it is in the air is called a *volley.* Hitting a ball after it has bounced once is called a *ground stroke.* Ground strokes are usually made with a *forehand* or a *backhand drive.* The forehand is a stroke made by holding the racket out to the side of the body. A backhand drive is made by reaching across the body. After the serve is returned, the players hit the ball back and forth until someone wins a point.

A form of tennis was played in France during the Middle Ages. Modern tennis was first played in England in 1873. The first major tennis competition was held at Wimbledon, England, in 1877. Today, Wimbledon is still the world's best-known tennis tournament.

Tennis has many star players. In recent years, top men players have included Rod Laver of Australia, Bjorn Borg of Sweden, and John McEnroe of the United States. Billie Jean King, Chris Evert, and Martina Navratilova are among the well-known recent women tennis stars. (*See* **Evert, Chris.**)

Tennis has grown as a sport since the late 1960s. In 1968, the U.S. tennis championships were opened to professional players for the first time. During the 1970s, television coverage of major tournaments made more people tennis fans and encouraged many people to play tennis themselves.

termite

The termite is a small, colorless insect. Some termites look like white ants. But a termite has a thick waist, while an ant has a narrow waist. Termites are more closely related to cockroaches than to ants.

Many kinds of termites feed on wood. They cannot digest the wood, but one-celled organisms in their intestines can. The organisms break down the wood into substances the termites can use.

Termites live in large colonies. A colony may contain several million termites. These form three groups called *castes.* A few of the termites are kings and queens. Their job is to reproduce. They are the only termites with wings. Soldiers form the second caste. They defend the colony. The third caste is made up of workers. Most members of a colony are workers. They build and repair the nest, gather food, and do other chores.

Some kinds of termites build nests in the ground, tunneling deep into the soil. Sometimes, these nests extend aboveground and rise as high as 6 meters (20 feet). Other termites live in wood. They often are serious pests. They do a lot of damage by tunneling into wooden buildings, telephone poles, furniture, books, and other items.

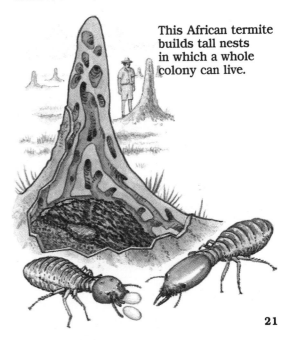

This African termite builds tall nests in which a whole colony can live.

Texas

Capital: Austin
Area: 266,807 square miles (691,030 square kilometers) (2nd-largest state)
Population (1980): 14,227,799 (1985): about 16,370,000 (3rd-largest state)
Became a state: December 29, 1845 (28th state)

Texas is a very large state in the southwestern United States. Of all the states, only Alaska is larger.

Texas is bordered on the south by Mexico and the Gulf of Mexico. In the northwestern part of Texas, a section of land known as the "Panhandle" reaches north to Oklahoma. Arkansas and Louisiana are in the east and New Mexico is to the west.

Land Texas is separated from Mexico by the Rio Grande. It is the largest river in the state, and one of the largest in North America. (*See* **Rio Grande.**)

Texas is so large that it has a variety of landscapes and climates, but most of the state is made up of plains. The highest point in Texas is Guadalupe Peak. It rises 8,749 feet (2,667 meters) above sea level.

The central part of Texas has the mildest climate. The northern Panhandle is the coldest area. Daytime temperatures throughout the state can get very hot.

The plains and grasslands of Texas are perfect for farming and ranching. The state is also rich in natural resources. About half of all the known oil and gas in the United States lies buried under Texan soil. Texas leads all the other states in the production of oil, cattle, sheep, cotton, and minerals.

History Indians lived in the region long before Spanish explorers arrived during the 1500s. Spanish colonists and missionaries built settlements in the late 1600s. When Mexico declared its independence from Spain in 1821, Texas became part of the new nation.

Spain, and later Mexico, gave Americans permission to settle in Texas during the 1820s. The Americans became unhappy living under Mexican rule and declared their freedom in 1835. In 1836, at a fortified mission in San Antonio called the Alamo, every Texan defender was killed, including Davy Crockett and Jim Bowie. That same year,

NEW MEXICO

Guadalupe Peak (8,751 ft.)

El Paso

Pecos

PICTURESQUE MEXICAN BORDER CITY, DATING TO TIME OF SPANISH CONQUISTADORES

▲ Historical Sites and Points of Interest

General Sam Houston captured the Mexican general Santa Anna at the Battle of San Jacinto. This battle ended the war. Houston was elected first president of the Republic of Texas. In 1845, Texas joined the United States. (*See* **Houston, Sam.**)

Texans fought Mexico again during the Mexican War, from 1846 to 1848. Mexico lost the war and was forced to give up all claims to Texas. During the Civil War, Texas left the United States and joined the Confederate States of America. When the South lost, Texas came back into the Union. (*See* **Mexican War** and **Civil War.**)

As the population of Texas grew, farmers planted cotton, and ranchers raised cattle. The cattle were called *longhorns,* because the distance between the tips of their horns could be as much as 6 feet (1.8 meters). Starting in the 1860s, cowboys drove the longhorns to markets in Kansas along the Chisholm Trail. The building of railroads made the cattle drives unnecessary by the end of the 1880s.

Borger

Amarillo

OKLAHOMA

Red *River*

BIRTHPLACE OF DWIGHT
D. EISENHOWER (34th
president of the U.S.)

Mockingbird

Plainview

Wichita Falls

Lake
Texoma

Denison

Paris

Texarkana

Levelland
Lubbock

Brazos *River*

Sherman

Denton

PRESIDENT
JOHN F. KENNEDY
ASSASSINATED, 1963

Longview

Marshall

Lamesa

Abilene

Fort Worth

Cleburne

Dallas

Tyler

Corsicana

Big Spring

Colorado

TEXAS

SOUTHERN
METHODIST
UNIVERSITY

Palestine

Sabine *River*

LOUISIANA

Midland

Odessa

San Angelo

River

Waco

Lufkin

Sam Rayburn
Reservoir

Pecos *River*

Killeen

Temple

GENERAL SAM
HOUSTON'S HOME

Huntsville

SPINDLETOP
MONUMENT
(site of oil field
discovered in
1901)

Bluebonnet

LBJ RANCH (home of
Lyndon B. Johnson, 36th
president of the U.S.)

Austin

SAN JACINTO BATTLEFIELD
(Mexicans defeated by
Houston's forces, 1836)

Beaumont
Port
Arthur

Del Rio
Reservoir

RANDOLPH
OIL FIELD

Baytown

Galveston
Bay

MEXICO

Del Rio

San Antonio

SITE OF LYNDON B.
JOHNSON SPACE
CENTER

Houston

Galveston
Texas City

"THE ALAMO" (where
Texans made their last
stand against the
Mexicans, 1836)

Victoria

Bay City

Matagorda
Bay

Oil storage tanks
near Houston.

Rio *Grande*

Nueces *River*

KING RANCH (largest
in Texas, almost
1 million acres)

Aransas
Bay

Gulf *of* *Mexico*

ELEVATION Feet

7000-10000
5000-7000
3000-5000
2000-3000
1500-2000
1000-1500
600-1000
300-600
0-300

0 Miles 100

Laredo

Corpus
Christi

Kingsville

Laguna
Madre

McAllen Harlingen
Brownsville

People Almost one out of five Texans is of Mexican or Spanish descent. More than three-fourths of all Texans live in cities. Several million people make their homes in or near the cities of Houston and Galveston. These cities are centers of the oil and gas industry. Houston is also the home of the Johnson Space Center, headquarters of NASA's manned space program. The Space Center is named for Texan Lyndon B. Johnson, 36th president of the United States.

The Dallas–Fort Worth area, in the northeastern part of the state, also has several million people. Dallas is a commercial, financial, and transportation center. Fort Worth is a center of the cattle industry.

Austin, the state capital, is in east-central Texas. Its factories manufacture electronic equipment, glass, and furniture.

Thailand

Capital: Bangkok
Area: 198,456 square miles (514,000 square kilometers)
Population (1985): about 51,546,000
Official language: Thai

Thailand (TY-land) is a large country in southeastern Asia. It has a large northern part and a long thin tail stretching south. Thailand has about as much land as North Carolina, South Carolina, Georgia, and Florida put together. It has about twice as many people as these four states. From 1782 to 1939, the nation was known as Siam.

Thailand is a part of the Indochinese Peninsula—a landmass that juts south from Asia between the Bay of Bengal and the Gulf of Thailand. Other countries on the Indochinese Peninsula are Burma, Laos, Cambodia, and Vietnam.

Thailand is just north of the equator and has warm weather year-round. The rugged mountains of the north and west receive heavy rains. The forests produce teak and other valuable trees. Few people live in these regions. Most Thais live in river valleys in the central part of the country. This region has rich soil, receives plenty of moisture, and is good for farming. The main crop is rice.

Bangkok is the capital and the most important business center. It is near the Gulf of Thailand on the Chao Phraya, one of Thailand's major rivers. Bangkok has more than 5 million people.

People were living in what is now Thailand more than 5,000 years ago. By the year 1000, peoples from the north had settled in the region. These settlers brought the Buddhist religion with them. Most Thais today are Buddhists.

In the 1600s, the Thais fought wars with their neighbors and seized land from the Burmese. The Thais were the most powerful people in Indochina. In the 1800s, the countries of Europe wanted colonies in Southeast Asia. Thai leaders never agreed to make Thailand a colony, but they did give European traders some special rights. In the middle 1800s, King Mongkut sent his son to

A line of Buddha statues inside a Buddhist temple in Thailand.

Europe to study. Later, the boy became King Chulalongkorn. Like his father, Chulalongkorn would not let the Europeans take over Thailand. He abolished slavery in Thailand and set up public schools.

In 1941, during World War II, Thailand was captured by Japan. Japan was defeated in 1945, and Thailand became independent again. During the 1960s and 1970s, there were many wars in Indochina, but none in Thailand. Thailand received many *refugees* —people fleeing from other countries. Today, most Thais live simply, but they have a higher standard of living than most other peoples of Asia.

Thanksgiving

Thanksgiving is a national holiday in the United States and Canada. It is a day when people give thanks for all the good things they have in life. Families celebrate Thanksgiving by offering prayers and preparing large dinners for their relatives and friends.

One of the first Thanksgiving celebrations in North America was held in 1621 by a group of settlers called the Pilgrims. They had landed in North America in 1620 and founded Plymouth Colony in Massachusetts. More than half of them died from starvation and sickness during the first winter. That spring, Indians taught the Pilgrims to plant corn, beans, and squash. The summer of 1621 brought a rich harvest.

The colony's governor, William Bradford, declared that some time should be set aside that fall for giving thanks to God. The Pilgrims and Indians prepared a large feast. At this first Thanksgiving, they served turkey, fish, fruit, and vegetables. (*See* **Pilgrims** and **Plymouth**.)

The idea of celebrating Thanksgiving soon spread to other colonies. Each settlement held its Thanksgiving on a different day. In 1789, soon after taking office as the first president, George Washington declared that November 26 of that year should be celebrated as a day of national thanksgiving.

In the years after 1789, there was still no specific day set aside for celebrating Thanksgiving. Then Sarah Josepha Hale, the editor of a popular women's magazine, urged President Abraham Lincoln to declare a national Thanksgiving holiday. In 1863, President Lincoln decided that Thanksgiving ought to be celebrated on the last Thursday in November.

Each year after that, the president of the United States would declare the last Thursday in November to be Thanksgiving Day. In 1941, Congress named the fourth Thursday in November as the official national day for Thanksgiving. In Canada, Thanksgiving is always celebrated on the second Monday in October.

Turkey has become a traditional Thanksgiving food in many families. Cranberries, apples, sweet potatoes, bread stuffing for the turkey, and pumpkin pie are also Thanksgiving favorites. Yet many families have their own special dishes and their own ways of celebrating. In some American cities, parades and football games have become part of the celebration.

Thanksgiving celebrations often include a dinner of roast turkey.

theater, *see* play; actors and acting

theme park

A theme park is an amusement park organized around a specific idea. They are entertaining and often educational places for people of all ages to enjoy throughout the year.

Some theme parks are built around historical themes. Colonial Williamsburg in Virginia re-creates the early American town as it looked during the 1700s. Mystic Seaport in Connecticut has old sailing ships and a re-created 1700s seaport.

Other theme parks are about modern life or about the world of the future. The Alabama Space and Rocket Center is a modern-day theme park where visitors learn

Disney World in Florida and Disneyland in California are popular theme parks.

about space travel. At Opryland USA in Tennessee, American music is celebrated in sections devoted to country, folk, jazz, western, and pop. Sea World in California and Ocean World in Florida allow visitors to see dolphins and whales perform. Other exhibits feature sharks, penguins, turtles, and different kinds of fish.

The largest and most popular theme parks in the world are Disneyland in California and Walt Disney World in Florida. Both of these enormous parks include a Magic Kingdom that is made up of several different "lands," such as Adventureland and Tomorrowland. (*See* **Disney, Walt.**)

See also **Williamsburg.**

theory

In science, a theory is an explanation based on many observations. One example is the cell theory. It states that all living things are made of cells that carry on certain life activities and reproduce to make new cells. This theory grew out of thousands of observations made by scientists over two centuries. As scientists continue to study living things, they are making more observations that support the cell theory.

Theories are ideas based on facts, but theories are not facts themselves. Theories change when new observations contradict the theories, or when new explanations fit the facts better. Sir Isaac Newton's theory of gravity, published in 1687, explained almost all the facts observed by astronomers about how planets move. But it failed to explain one fact about how the planet Mercury moved. In 1915, Albert Einstein developed a new theory of gravity, called the *general theory of relativity.* It explained the orbit of Mercury and predicted that gravity would affect light in a certain way. In 1919, this prediction was found to be true. Since then, scientists who must make careful measurements have used Einstein's theory.

See also **scientific method; hypothesis; and experiment.**

thermometer

A thermometer is an instrument used to measure temperature. The most common type is the *liquid-in-glass thermometer*. It contains liquid sealed inside a glass tube. When the liquid is heated, it expands and rises up the tube. When cooled, it contracts and falls down the tube. The distance the liquid moves is measured on a temperature scale, which is printed on the tube. (*See* **temperature scale.**)

Liquid-in-glass thermometers usually contain alcohol mixed with a dye to make the liquid easier to see. Medical liquid-in-glass thermometers contain mercury, which is more accurate.

Another type of thermometer, a *bimetallic thermometer,* contains two kinds of metal strips that contract and expand at different rates when the temperature changes. The strips are joined into one thin coil. One end of the coil is attached to a frame. The other end is often attached to a dial on which the temperature can be read.

A *digital thermometer* is one on which the temperature can be read in numbers. Most digital thermometers have tiny electronic devices that can turn changes of temperature into electrical signals.

**Three kinds of thermometers:
the digital thermometer (left top),
the bimetallic thermometer (left bottom),
and the liquid thermometer (right).**

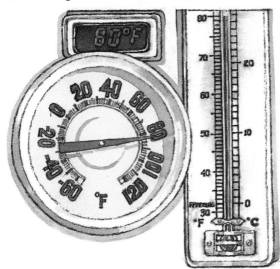

Jim Thorpe, an American Indian, won an Olympic decathlon and played pro football.

Thorpe, Jim

Most athletes are good at one sport. Jim Thorpe was great at many. Some sports fans think that he was the best athlete ever.

Thorpe, an American Indian, was born in 1888 in what is now Oklahoma. He went to a school for Indians in Pennsylvania. He led the school's football team to many victories. In the summer, he earned a few dollars playing baseball.

In 1912, Thorpe competed in the Olympic Games in Sweden. He won a gold medal in the *decathlon,* which is a series of ten running, throwing, and jumping events. He also won a gold medal in the *pentathlon,* a series of five events. A few months later, Olympic officials took away Thorpe's medals. They said that he had broken Olympic rules when he accepted money for playing baseball. Thorpe believed that the officials were being unfair. Many people agreed with him.

After the Olympics, Thorpe became a major league baseball player. He later played professional football, and was elected to the Pro Football Hall of Fame.

Jim Thorpe died in 1953. Twenty years later, Olympic officials restored his 1912 amateur standing and returned his gold medals to his family.

Electrical charges in water droplets create conditions for a thunderstorm.

thunderstorm

A thunderstorm is a rainstorm with both lightning and thunder. It has three stages. In the first stage, warm, moist air rises. Up high, it cools and forms thunderclouds of ice crystals and water droplets.

At the *mature* stage, the thunderclouds may tower 21,300 meters (70,000 feet). Water droplets and ice crystals begin to fall. As they fall, they develop a negative electric charge. The lighter, rising drops in the cloud develop a positive charge. Lightning streaks between the opposite charges. The lightning's heat makes the air expand suddenly. The expanding air crashes into the surrounding air and makes a loud boom—the thunder. The cloud seems to burst. Heavy rains and sometimes hail pelt down.

During the *final* stage, no moist air is rising. The rain or hail stops and the clouds disappear.

Light travels faster than sound, so you see the lightning before you hear the thunder. You can figure your distance from a thunderstorm by counting the seconds between the lightning and the rumble. To find the distance in kilometers, divide the number of seconds by three. To find the distance in miles, divide the number of seconds by five.

See also **cloud; hail; lightning; tornado;** and **weather.**

Tibet, *see* China

tick

A tick is a tiny animal that looks like an insect. But ticks are *arachnids*—members of a group of animals that also includes spiders. Arachnids have four pairs of legs, while insects have three pairs of legs.

Ticks are *parasites*—animals that live on or in another animal. The animal they live on is called the *host*. A tick attaches itself to the skin of a host by hanging on with its strong legs. The tick's long snout is covered with sharp, hooked barbs. The mouth is at the end of the snout. The tick pierces the host's skin with its snout and feeds on the blood. As it feeds, it gets bigger. When it has finished eating, it may be 2.5 centimeters (1 inch) across.

A tick will stay attached to its host for hours, weeks, or until the host dies. If a tick drops off its host, it can still live for a long time. Some dog ticks have stayed alive without food for three years!

Ticks are serious pests, because they spread diseases. Rocky Mountain spotted fever, Lyme disease, and tularemia are three serious human diseases that are spread by ticks. Ticks also spread tularemia and many other diseases to animals.

Ticks live almost everywhere but are most common in warm, tropical lands. Tick populations may grow rapidly. Female ticks lay thousands of eggs at a time.

A tick shown at life size— before and after eating!

At low tide on Canada's Bay of Fundy, people walk along a gently sloping beach.
At high tide, the water level may be 40 feet higher than at low tide.

tide

Every day, where oceans meet the land, the water level rises and falls. This rising and falling motion is called the tide. In most parts of the world, the sea slowly rises for about 6 hours. Then, after it reaches high tide, it drops back down over another 6 hours, until it reaches low tide. In 24 hours and 50 minutes, the sea rises twice and it falls twice.

The difference in height between high and low tides is called the *tidal range*. In some places, the tidal range is very small. But in a few places, the range is especially large. In Nova Scotia's Bay of Fundy, for example, the difference between high tide and low is as much as 15 meters (50 feet). These differences are caused mainly by the shape of the ocean bottom.

Tides are important to sailors and fishermen, and to anyone who lives near the sea. In some harbors, the water is not deep enough for a ship to sail out to sea until high tide. If you know the schedule of the tides, you know when your ship must be ready to sail. You also would not build your house so close to the ocean that it would be flooded by the high tide.

Long ago, people figured out that the regular rise and fall of the tides was somehow connected with the moon. But they were not able to explain what caused the tides until the 1600s, when Sir Isaac Newton discovered how gravity works. He saw that the gravitational forces of the sun and the moon combined to pull on Earth's waters, causing the tides.

Whenever high tide comes to one side of the earth, it also comes to the opposite side of the earth. The side facing the moon has high tide, because this is where the moon's gravity is pulling the strongest. The side farthest from the moon has high tide, too, because the moon's gravity pulls the solid Earth away from the liquid ocean.

The sun, too, pulls on Earth's water, but only half as hard as the moon does, because the sun is so much farther away. When the sun, moon, and Earth are all in the same line, the high tides are higher than at any other time of year. These are called *spring tides*. When the sun, Earth, and moon form a right angle, the high tides are unusually low. This is because the moon and sun are pulling in different directions. These are called *neap tides*.

See also tideland.

tideland

Tideland is the area found along oceans. It is covered by seawater when the tide is high, and exposed to the air when the tide is low. There are two high tides and two low tides every day. (*See* **tide.**)

Few living things are able to survive a tideland's harsh environment. The ones that do have adapted in fascinating ways to cope with living on land and in salt water. Many tideland animals have coverings that keep them from drying out when the water is low. Barnacles have shells that close tight. Starfish have thick skins that protect them. Worms and razor clams burrow into the wet sand. Other animals hide between rocks.

Some animals feed when the tide goes out. Crabs and some worms eat the matter left behind by the water. On sandy beaches, some animals feed on the bacteria and tiny algae that grow on the grains of sand.

Other animals feed when the tide comes in. The water that covers the tideland is rich in food. Barnacles and mussels open their shells to filter food from the water.

When the tide goes out, it creates a strong pull. Animals that live in tidelands anchor themselves so that they are not washed out to sea. In rocky areas, large algae attach themselves to the rocks with rootlike structures called *holdfasts.* Starfish cling to rocks by their tube feet. Barnacles produce a strong glue that permanently cements them to the rocks. Mussels hold on by strings they make. Other animals get into rock crevices as the water goes out.

In some tidelands, pools of water stay filled even when the tide goes out. Tide pools are especially common in rocky areas. Many insects live in tide pools. You may also see tiny crabs and fish. Threads of red and green algae grow in these pools. In warm areas, sea anemones live attached to the pool's rocks.

This starfish and crab live in tidelands, together with many other living things.

tiger

The tiger is the largest member of the cat family. Its beautiful yellow-orange or red-orange fur has black stripes. An average-size male weighs about 190 kilograms (420 pounds). Females are smaller.

Tigers live in forests. The Siberian tiger, which is very rare, lives in cold, snowy forests in northern Asia. Most other tigers live

in tropical forests. On hot days, tigers like to take baths to cool off.

Like all cats, tigers are *carnivores*—meat-eaters. Hoofed animals such as deer, antelope, and cattle are their main prey. They will also eat fish, frogs, monkeys, and anything else they can catch. A few tigers have been known to attack people, but most tigers avoid people.

Tigers may hunt during the day, perhaps by lying in wait for animals at a water hole. But they usually hunt at night. They depend mostly on their excellent eyesight and hearing to find prey. Sometimes, a tiger does not catch anything for several days or even a week. Hoofed animals are very watchful, and quick to run away when they sense a tiger's presence. Even though a tiger is so large, it can move very quietly. Slowly, it moves close to the prey. Then it leaps. The tiger forces the animal to the ground and bites it in the neck or throat. After killing its prey, the tiger drags the body to a sheltered spot and eats until it is full. A tiger can eat up to 23 kilograms (50 pounds) of meat at one meal! If it catches a large animal, such as a horse, it

The Siberian tiger (left) lives in the cold north. Bengal tigers (below and right) live in tropical forests.

will stay near the body for several days, resting and eating again, until nothing is left but bones.

Female tigers give birth to two or three cubs. At birth, the cubs are helpless. The mother keeps them hidden in a dense part of the forest until they are about six weeks old. Then they begin to follow her on her travels. The cubs stay with her until they are about two years old. By then, they have learned how to hunt alone.

At one time, tigers were found in much of Asia, from Turkey in the west to China and Korea in the east. But people killed many tigers and cut down the forests where tigers lived. Today, tigers are endangered. (*See* **animals, endangered.**)

See also **cat family.**

timberline

The timberline is the place on the side of a high mountain where the forest ends. There are no trees above the timberline, just bare, rocky slopes with a few small plants. These plants are the same kinds that grow on *tundras*—treeless plains that cover large areas of the Arctic north, such as Siberia, northern Canada, and northern Alaska. Trees growing just below the timberline are twisted and even stunted.

Mountain climbers know that the higher they climb, the thinner and cooler the air becomes. They get out of breath easily because there is not much oxygen. Even on mountains near the equator, they must dress warmly. Trees cannot grow much above 3,350 meters (11,000 feet). The temperatures at that height stay too low all year, and there is not enough carbon dioxide for the trees to carry on *photosynthesis.* This is a process that uses energy from the sun to make sugar from carbon dioxide and water. (*See* **photosynthesis.**)

See also **mountain** and **tundra.**

The shadow cast by a sundial's pointer shows the correct hour.

time and timetelling

Time is a way of measuring the period between one event and another. We have many ways of measuring time. We divide it into the past, the present, and the future. The past is what has gone by. The present is right now. The future is what will come.

Time is measured in days, weeks, months, years, decades, and centuries. It is also divided into hours, minutes, and seconds. The ways people think of time and measure time have changed throughout history.

Days, Weeks, Months Ancient peoples used what they saw in nature to tell time. Each morning, the sun rose in the sky. At sunset, the sky grew dark. The period from one sunrise to the next came to be called a *day.* (*See* **day and night.**)

People also noticed that the moon went through different *phases*—stages. At first, it appeared to be a thin sliver in the night sky. This was called the *new moon.* Each night the moon seemed to grow a little bigger. Finally, it was a complete circle. This was called the *full moon.* Each night after that, the moon seemed to get a little bit smaller. Every 29 ½ days, these phases would be repeated. People referred to the time between one new moon and the next as a *moon,* or *month.* (*See* **month.**)

Early humans also grouped days into sevens. Seven days are a *week,* and there are about four weeks in each month. The idea of seven days making up a week is not based on any scientific idea about time. The Bible says that God created the heavens and the earth in six days and rested on the seventh day. One of the Ten Commandments is about observing the seventh day as the Sabbath, a special day for worship and rest. Jews, Christians, and Muslims all divide time into weeks of seven days and observe one of the days as special. (*See* **week.**)

The Year The passing seasons were another way that people measured time. In some parts of the world, cold weather and warm weather came and went in a regular pattern. In other regions, some periods were rainy and others were dry. People divided time into seasons in order to know when to plant crops and when to expect them to be ready for harvest.

Changes in weather were connected with changes in the length of day and night. When days were longest, the weather was usually the warmest and crops would grow. When days were shortest, the weather might be much colder. After the longest day of summer, days would gradually become shorter. The shortest day occurred about 183 days later. Then days gradually got longer again. About 365 days passed between the longest day of one summer and the longest day of the next summer. People called this period a *year.* (*See* **year.**)

Early astronomers saw different star groups—*constellations*—at different times of year. These changes in the night sky helped people keep track of the changing seasons.

Early humans held many of their festivals and religious ceremonies at the time of the *equinoxes*—the two days each year when night and day are exactly the same length. Today, we know the equinoxes as the first day of spring (around March 21) and the first day of fall (around September 21). Other ceremonies were held around the *solstices*. North of the equator, the winter solstice is the shortest day of the year (around December 21). The summer solstice is the longest day of the year (around June 21).

Measuring the year was so important to some peoples that they built special structures to help them. These were the first *observatories*—places from which people could study the stars and the planets. (*See* **observatory** and **Stonehenge.**)

People who studied the stars and planets noticed that these heavenly bodies change positions slightly each night. Some groups of stars slipped below the horizon for a while. Then they would come back. It took a full year for the sky to look the same again.

Big Measures of Time　Ten years make a decade. One hundred years make a *century.* The initials *A.D.* sometimes appear before the name of a year. They stand for the Latin words *anno Domini,* "the year of the Lord." For centuries before Christ's birth, we use the initials *B.C.*—before Christ.

Each century begins with a year that ends in the numeral 1. The 20th century began in the year 1901. The last year of the century is 2000. The 21st century begins in 2001.

Scientists measure time in even larger units. Those who study early humans measure by thousands of years. A thousand years is a *millennium.* Those who study the earth and the stars measure in millions of years. Some scientists believe that the earth itself is more than 4 billion—4,000 million —years old.

Hours, Minutes, Seconds　Nearly 3,000 years ago in Babylonia, astronomers wanted smaller units to mark off day and night. They decided to divide the period between sunrise and sunset into 12 equal parts. They did the same for the period between sunset and sunrise. These 24 periods became known as *hours.*

They soon saw a problem—the hours could not all be of equal length. In the summer, daytime was longer than nighttime. This meant that daytime hours had to be longer than nighttime hours. In the winter, nighttime was longer than daytime, so the nighttime hours had to be longer.

Later, a Greek astronomer named Hipparchus decided that each day should have 24 equal hours, no matter when the sun rose and set. He used this timetelling system to measure when the sun rose and set at different times of year. He also measured when certain planets and stars seemed to rise and set.

Ptolemy was another Greek scientist. He went a step further, and divided each hour into 60 equal minutes, and each minute into 60 equal seconds. More than 1000 years later, in the 1300s, the first mechanical clocks were made. The people who built them used Ptolemy's system of hours, minutes, and seconds.

Today, scientists can measure time periods that are much smaller than a second. Even inexpensive watches can break down the second into hundredths. Scientists and computer technicians often measure time in *milliseconds*—thousandths of a second. They also measure in *nanoseconds*—millionths of a second.

Clock Time When people began making mechanical clocks in the 1300s, they used Ptolemy's system of hours, minutes, and seconds. They made a round clock face showing 12 hours. The hour hand of the clock takes one hour to move from one number to the next. Each day, the hour hand goes around the face of the clock two times. The two parts of the day are often called A.M. and P.M. The abbreviation A.M. stands for the Latin words *ante meridiem,* which means "before noon." P.M. stands for *post meridiem,* another Latin phrase, which means "after noon." A.M. begins just after midnight, and P.M. begins just after noon.

The minute hand of the clock goes around the face 24 times each day—once each hour. It takes exactly five minutes for the minute hand to move from one hour number to the next.

Some clocks have a second hand that goes around the face 60 times an hour—once each minute. It takes five seconds for the second hand to move from one number on the clock face to the next.

Some countries, scientists, and military groups follow a 24-hour clock. Under this system, the day starts at 12:00 midnight. The hours are numbered 0 through 24. Midnight is 000, and noon is 1200. The hour following noon is called 1300. The minute before midnight is 2359.

The pull of a weight and the regular swing of a pendulum run the antique clock (top). The hour hand of the electric 24-hour clock (above) goes around only once each day. The electric digital clock (below) has no face, telling time in numbers instead.

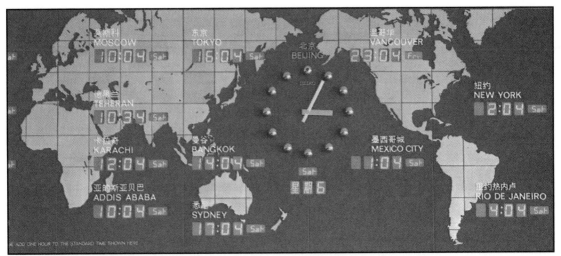

This board in the airport at Beijing, China, shows the world's time zones. At 3:04 in the afternoon in Beijing, it is 2:04 in the morning in New York City.

Time Zones For centuries, people in each town and city kept their own time. But when travel and communication became faster and easier, it became clear that some kind of system was needed. When the sun is at its highest point in New York, it is the middle of the night in China. If you try to call an office in China then, there will be no answer, because people are at home asleep.

Today, the world is divided into 24 time zones. Each zone is about the same size. When you are traveling west, you set your watch back one hour when you cross into a new time zone. When you are traveling east, you set your watch ahead one hour each time you cross into a new time zone.

We need to know about the time zones when we make long-distance phone calls. For example, a child in Pennsylvania would not want to call a grandparent in California at 8:00 A.M. It is only 5:00 A.M. in California—too early for most people to be awake!

In the middle of the Pacific Ocean, there is one especially important boundary between time zones. It is called the *international date line.* When people cross this line, they must change not only their watches but also their calendars. West of the date line, it is one day later. If people cross from east to west, they are moving ahead a day. If they are crossing west to east, they are moving back to yesterday, since it is a day earlier. (*See* **international date line.**)

See also **measurement; calendar;** and **clock.**

tin

Tin is a white metal and a chemical element. It is easily shaped and can be made into very thin foils and coatings. Steel cans have a thin coating of tin to protect them from the acids in foods and to keep the steel from rusting. Steel pins and staples are a few of the other steel products that are protected by a coating of tin.

Tin by itself is a weak metal. More often, it is combined with other metals to make alloys that resist *corrosion*—destruction by other elements and compounds. Around 3500 B.C., people combined it with copper to make bronze—the earliest known alloy. Tin is combined with lead to make solder. Melted solder is used to join pieces of metal. Pewter is an alloy of tin, copper, and antimony. Pewter has a dull, silvery luster—shine—and is used for plates and mugs. (*See* **bronze.**)

Large deposits of tin ores exist in Malaysia, Bolivia, Indonesia, Thailand, and Brazil.

toad, *see* frogs and toads

tobacco

Tobacco is a plant related to the tomato and potato plants. It grows from 120 to 180 centimeters (4 to 6 feet) tall and produces about 20 large leaves. The leaves are dried, cured, aged, and shredded to make smoking tobacco for cigarettes, cigars, and pipes. Some tobacco is made into snuff, which is inhaled, or into chewing tobacco. Chemicals from tobacco are used in fertilizers, disinfectants, and insecticides.

Tobacco contains nicotine, a chemical that stimulates the nervous system and heart. Some people enjoy this effect, but using tobacco leads to nicotine *addiction.* The body comes to depend on having the nicotine. The addiction makes it hard for people to stop smoking. Furthermore, chemicals in tobacco cause lung cancer, heart disease, and other diseases. Many countries, including the United States, put health warning labels on tobacco products so that people who use tobacco know they are risking serious disease. (*See* **addiction**.)

American Indians smoked tobacco in pipes long before Europeans arrived in North America. The settlers learned to use and grow tobacco. They shipped it to Europe, where tobacco use also gained popularity before people learned of its dangers.

A worker in North Carolina harvests tobacco leaves by hand.

Togo, *see* Africa

Tokyo

Tokyo (TOE-kee-o) is Japan's capital and largest city. With a population of about 9 million, Tokyo is one of the world's ten largest cities.

Tokyo is on the shore of Honshu Island, the largest island of Japan. To the east is Tokyo Bay, an arm of the Pacific Ocean. Tokyo is one of Japan's most important ports.

To the west of Tokyo is a high range of mountains that were once active volcanoes. The most famous is Mount Fujiyama, which rises 12,388 feet (3,716 meters) above sea level. On a clear day, its snowcapped peak can be seen from downtown Tokyo. Every year, thousands of people climb to the top of the great mountain.

The city was founded sometime after the year 1000. In the 1600s, it became the capital of the Tokugawas, a group of *shoguns* —warlords. These powerful military lords ruled all of Japan.

In 1867, people who wanted a more modern government overthrew the Tokugawas. They put an emperor on the throne, but also arranged for elected leaders to make many government decisions. This was the beginning of the modern era in Japan.

Today, Tokyo has only a few ancient buildings. In 1923, about half of the city was destroyed by an earthquake and fire. New buildings soon went up. In World War II, during the 1940s, Japan was at war against the United States. U.S. bombers attacked Tokyo. Much of the city was destroyed, including most of its factories.

In 1945, Japan surrendered. The United States, which had been an enemy, then became a friend. The U.S. government contributed to rebuilding Japan's damaged cities and factories. Tokyo was soon one of the world's largest and most important cities.

Millions of people travel into Tokyo each day to work. Many ride *monorails*—trains

A main intersection in downtown Tokyo. The city is the center of Japanese business and government. It is one of the most interesting and exciting cities in the world.

that run on a single track. The Tokyo subway system is one of the busiest in the world. In addition, high-speed "bullet trains," which can travel more than 200 miles (320 kilometers) per hour, connect Tokyo with other large cities.

Tokyo is Japan's center of business and education. Most major Japanese companies have their headquarters in Tokyo. Factories in or near the city produce electronic goods, automobiles, and other products. There are more than 100 universities.

tomato

The tomato is a round, juicy fruit that grows on vines. Ripe tomatoes are usually red, but some are pink or yellow. Tomatoes are related to potatoes. Scientists call tomatoes fruits because they have seeds. Yet most people think of tomatoes as vegetables because they are not very sweet.

Tomatoes are eaten raw in salads and sandwiches. They are also processed and cooked in many ways. Most tomatoes grown in the United States are canned or made into juice, soup, sauce, ketchup, or tomato paste. Tomato sauces are poured over spaghetti and pizza, and are used in many meat and

fish dishes. Tomatoes picked while they are green may be pickled or fried.

Tomatoes come in many sizes and shapes. Small tomatoes are known as *cherry tomatoes*. Egg-shaped tomatoes are often called *plum tomatoes*. The largest tomatoes are called *beefsteak tomatoes*.

Tomatoes are annuals—they go through their life cycle in one season. In warm climates in the spring, the tomato seeds are planted outdoors. In cooler areas, the seeds are started indoors. When the danger of frost

Tomatoes may be preserved by pickling, or made into sauces and bottled.

is over, the seedlings are replanted outside. In the summer, the tomato plants bear small, yellow flowers and produce the fruits. By autumn frost, the vines have withered and died. Some tomatoes are grown indoors in greenhouses. (*See* **greenhouse.**)

The tomato is a favorite crop of home gardeners. They tie the vines to tall sticks called *stakes.* This makes it easier to remove weeds and keeps the fruit off the ground, where it can easily rot.

Farmers harvest large crops of tomatoes by machine before the tomatoes are completely ripe. This is because unripe tomatoes are not as quick to spoil or bruise when they are shipped. The tomatoes are sent to warehouses, where they are allowed to ripen.

Tomatoes are rich in vitamins A and C. They are also good for people who are watching their weight, because they are low in carbohydrates.

Tomatoes were first grown for food in Mexico, Central America, and the Andes Mountains of South America. Spanish explorers brought tomatoes to Europe around 1500. For many years, Europeans grew tomatoes only for decoration, not for food, because people thought they were poisonous. The Italians and Spanish were the first Europeans to use tomatoes as food. Today, tomatoes are a favorite food in many countries and one of the most important crops grown in the United States.

Tom Sawyer

Tom Sawyer is a character invented by Mark Twain, an American writer. Tom is a clever and mischievous 12-year-old who lives in a small Missouri town along the Mississippi River. He is the main character in *The Adventures of Tom Sawyer.* He also appears in *The Adventures of Huckleberry Finn.* Twain used his own boyhood experiences to create these books, which became favorites with children and grown-ups.

Beefsteak tomatoes ripen in the sun. The tomato fruit develops from the flower. Tomatoes on the same plant may ripen at different times.

Tom gets his friends to whitewash a fence. They even pay him for a chance to help!

The Adventures of Tom Sawyer was printed in 1876. The story takes place before the Civil War (1861 to 1865). Tom lives with his aunt Polly. His best friend is Huck Finn, and his sweetheart is Becky Thatcher. Tom tells fibs, plays pranks, and hates dressing up. He is also very shrewd. In one episode, Aunt Polly gives Tom the chore of painting her fence with whitewash. He makes this ordinary chore seem so special that the neighborhood boys beg to help. They even pay for the chance with their prized possessions— marbles, a key, a piece of blue glass, a piece of chalk, a brass doorknob, tadpoles, a kitten, a dog collar, and a knife handle. Tom becomes wealthy just sitting in the shade while the fence gets whitewashed.

Tom and Huck have exciting adventures. They try not to get caught by Aunt Polly or by Injun Joe—a man they saw murder the town's doctor.

See also **Twain, Mark.**

Tonga, *see* **Pacific Islands**

tonsils and adenoids

If you open your mouth wide and look in a mirror, you may be able to see your tonsils, unless they have been removed. The tonsils are masses of lymph tissue. They are located at either side of the back of the mouth. The adenoids, too, are composed of lymph tissue. They are found at the top of the throat. You cannot see the adenoids, because they are located behind the nose. Like the tonsils, the adenoids are sometimes removed. Both tonsils and adenoids naturally shrink in size after age six.

Lymph tissue contains cells that trap bacteria and other foreign bodies. Lymph tissue also contains many white blood cells. White blood cells produce chemicals that attack and destroy invading disease germs.

The tonsils and adenoids help prevent infection of the lungs and digestive system. But sometimes the tonsils and adenoids themselves become infected. Both have deep pits in which food and other material often get stuck. The lymph tissue then becomes infected and swollen. Often, the infection can be treated with drugs. If repeated infections occur, the tonsils or adenoids may need to be surgically removed. (*See* **surgery.**)

Tonsils are at the sides of the throat. Adenoids are in the passage between the nose and throat.

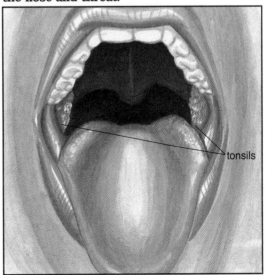

tonsils

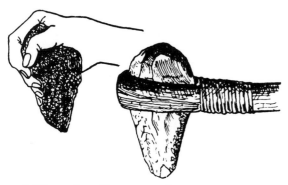

Adding a handle to a cutting stone created a tool that made work easier.

tool

A tool is any device used to help a person do something. Most tools are used for cutting, pounding, shaping, or changing an object in some other way. *Hand tools* are powered by the hand. All *power tools* are driven by motors. A machine that contains a power-driven tool for shaping metal is called a *machine tool.*

The earliest tools we have found were made about 2 million years ago. These were merely chipped stones. There may have been wooden tools earlier, but they have not survived. The chipped stones were later replaced by sharp stone axes, knives, and arrowheads. Later, people made other simple tools, including knives and needles, from animal bones or tusks. In the Bronze Age, people shaped tools from bronze, a mixture of copper and tin. In the Iron Age, people learned to fashion new and improved tools from iron and steel. With the introduction of steam and electrical power, power tools were developed. These provided great savings in time and effort.

Most tools can be put into one of six groups. They are grouped according to their function—measuring, cutting, shaping, drilling, fastening, and finishing.

Measuring tools include rulers, yardsticks, and tape measures. They are used to measure distances. Calipers measure very tiny distances. Compasses help in marking out circles. A square is used to create 90° angles. A bevel is used to mark out other angles.

Axes, hatchets, and saws are all *cutting tools.* Most cutting of wood is done with power saws. Power saws allow people to cut much faster than they could with handsaws.

Shaping tools include planes, chisels, and files. These tools shape and smooth wood or metal after it has been cut.

Drilling tools cut or grind holes through a material. Drills may be hand tools or power tools. In metalworking, machinists cut screw

Tools simplify many tasks.
Power tools can save time and effort.

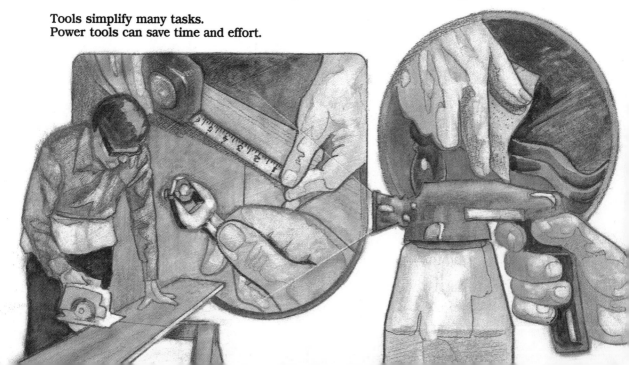

A tornado is among the most violent storms. This one has touched the ground. It is strong enough to pick up a farm building and carry it miles away.

threads inside holes with special drilling tools called *taps.*

Fastening tools join materials together with nails, screws, rivets, glue, or nuts and bolts. Hammers, screwdrivers, wrenches, and clamps are some hand fastening tools.

Finishing tools such as sandpaper and electric sanders smooth wood and other materials. Brushes, rollers, and pads are tools that apply finishes such as paint or varnish. Power-driven paint sprayers are used for very large painting jobs.

See also **machines, simple.**

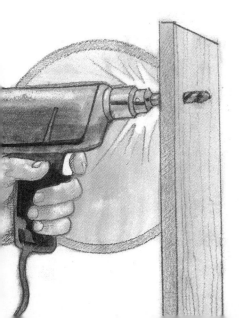

tornado

A tornado is a whirling, funnel-shaped cloud that hangs down from a black thundercloud. The funnel is made up of winds that swirl at up to 700 kilometers (450 miles) per hour. Hollow like a straw, the funnel sucks in everything it passes over. Dirt and dust trapped in the violent winds give the funnel its dark color.

Tornadoes usually occur in the spring and early summer. The hot sun bakes the land. In turn, the air close to the ground is heated by the land, and rises. Higher in the atmosphere, a cold air mass flows over the warm air mass. The cold air sinks. Dark clouds form. Due to large differences in temperature and air pressure between the warm and cold air, the air moves rapidly. As the warm air rises faster, air rushes in from all sides to take its place.

The inrushing air starts to spin in a circle. The winds closer to the center of the circle spin faster. Thunderstorms form. The spinning air extends down from the cloud in a funnel. The winds of such a funnel are the fiercest on earth. They roar and hiss as they sweep up everything in their path—rocks, cars, houses, and even people.

Like the eye of a hurricane, the air inside a funnel is calm. The air pressure in a tornado is much lower than the normal air pressure in any building it approaches. As a tornado passes over a building, the air inside the building presses outward against the roof and walls much harder than the air in the funnel presses inward. If the roof has not blown off, the force of the air pressure bursts the building like an overblown balloon.

Not all tornadoes touch down. Sometimes a tornado will dip to the earth, go back up into the air, and then dip down again.

Tornadoes strike most often in the midwestern United States. On these flat, open plains, no land barriers slow the movement of air masses.

A *waterspout* is a tornado over water. Instead of dirt, its whirling winds suck up water. A waterspout has the same shape as a land tornado, but it is not as powerful.

The average tornado topples buildings and uproots trees in a path 400 meters (¼ mile) wide and 18 kilometers (11 miles) long. It advances at 65 kilometers (40 miles) per hour and lasts about 15 minutes. Wider and longer-lasting tornadoes are not common, but they cause more damage. In 1925, a fast-moving tornado sprang up in Missouri and tore through Illinois and into Indiana. In 3 hours and 15 minutes, it traveled 352 kilometers (219 miles) and killed 689 people.

See also **thunderstorm; weather;** and **weather forecast.**

Toronto

Toronto is the capital of the Canadian province of Ontario. The city is located on the northwestern shore of Lake Ontario. It is linked to other cities on the Great Lakes and to the Atlantic Ocean by the St. Lawrence Seaway. This has helped to make it one of Canada's most important ports.

Toronto is a major center of industry and finance. Its factories make agricultural machinery, metal goods, clothing, and aircraft. There are large stockyards for cattle and

Toronto's city hall is next to a public square downtown.

hogs and many meat-packing plants. Several large companies have their headquarters in Toronto. Its stock exchange is the largest in Canada and one of the busiest in North America.

Toronto is also a major cultural and educational center. Canada's English-language printing and publishing industry is located there. Among the many universities in the city are the University of Toronto (the nation's largest) and York University.

Toronto began around 1720 as a French fur-trading post. Later, the French built a fort nearby to protect the trading post. The fort was burned down during the French and Indian War. The British and the French fought this war over northern and eastern North America from 1754 to 1763. Britain won the war and gained control of Canada. (*See* **French and Indian War.**)

In 1787, Britain bought the land where the fort had stood from the Missisauga Indians. The British established a settlement there and named it York, in honor of the duke of York, a son of King George III. The settlement grew quickly. In 1793, it was made the capital of the province of Upper Canada (present-day Ontario).

During the War of 1812, United States troops burned down some government buildings in York. In response, the British set fire to buildings in the U.S. capital, Washington, D.C. (*See* **War of 1812.**)

In 1834, York was renamed Toronto, an Indian word meaning "place of meeting." Toronto grew rapidly, both in population and area. By the middle 1900s, Toronto's metropolitan area had spread to include many neighboring communities.

To link all of these communities, Toronto adopted a new kind of metropolitan "supergovernment" in 1953. Under this system—called Metro—the central city and each community elects its own local officials. At the same time, each community also sends a representative to a metropolitan council. This council is in charge of providing the entire metropolitan area with certain public services—such as public transportation, police, water, and welfare.

In the late 1960s, Toronto began the largest downtown development project ever attempted in North America. It included a communications center and many new office and apartment buildings and hotels. In 1977, perhaps as a result of this project, Toronto's metropolitan-area population became the largest in Canada. Today, about 3,067,000 people live in and around the city of Toronto.

There are many interesting things to do and see in Toronto. The best-known landmark is the rocket-shaped CN Tower, near the lakeshore. The tower, 1,815 feet (553 meters) high, is the tallest freestanding building in the world. At the top is a revolving restaurant, where visitors can enjoy a meal and spectacular views.

Ontario Place is a recreation area built on man-made islands in Lake Ontario. It has movie theaters, outdoor concert stages, restaurants, and gift shops. It also includes Children's Village, which many people of all ages think is the best playground in the world.

Other places to visit include the Royal Ontario Museum, the Metro Toronto Zoo, and the Ontario Science Centre. In the summer, the Canadian National Exhibition, a large industrial and agricultural fair, is held on the Toronto lakefront.

Toronto also offers a wide variety of cultural and sporting events. The National Ballet of Canada and the Toronto Symphony Orchestra make their home in the city. Sports teams include the Toronto Maple Leafs hockey team and the Toronto Blue Jays baseball team.

Ontario Place, on the shore of Lake Ontario, is one of Toronto's many parks. Visitors may rent pedal boats to travel among artificial islands.

touch

Touch is the sense that lets you know when your body is in contact with something. The sense of touch also tells you about the object's temperature, hardness, softness, and shape.

Touch is usually considered just one sense, but it is actually made up of five different senses. When you press your hand lightly on an object, you feel it—that is *plain touch*. If you press harder, you sense *pressure*. If the object has a rough surface and you press hard enough, you feel *pain*. If the object is warm, you feel *warmth*. If the object is cold, you feel *cold*. Even though cold is just the absence of heat, the skin has different places where each is felt. Such places are called *receptors*. There are different kinds of

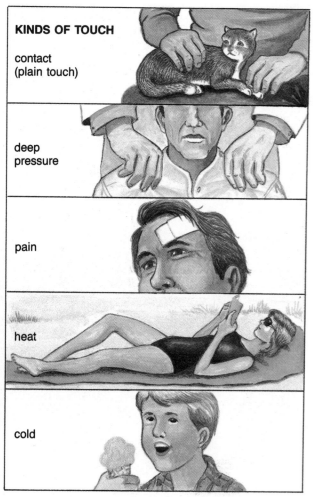

KINDS OF TOUCH

contact
(plain touch)

deep
pressure

pain

heat

cold

sense receptors in the skin for each of the five feelings.

The sense receptors are not spread out evenly over the whole body. Some areas have more sense receptors than other areas. The areas that have more sense receptors are more sensitive to touch. The most sensitive areas are the tip of the tongue, the tips of the fingers, and the tip of the nose. The sense receptors are very close together in these areas. The backs of the shoulders are less sensitive because the receptors are spaced farther apart.

The distance between touch receptors can be shown by measuring how far apart two pencil points have to be before they can be felt as two points. Gently touch two pencil points to the middle of someone's back. Then slowly move the points apart. On the average, the two points must be about 63 millimeters (2 1/2 inches) apart before they are felt as two points. On the forearm, they must be 38 millimeters (1 1/2 inches) apart. On the palm, the distance is 13 millimeters (1/2 inch). On the fingertip, it is 2.5 millimeters (1/10 inch).

Pain receptors are plentiful on the forehead, breast, and lower arm. On the forehead, there are 200 pain receptors in each square centimeter of skin. On the nose and thumb, there are only 50 receptors in each square centimeter.

Scientists can map the receptors for touch, pressure, pain, warmth, and cold on any area of the skin. Taking the body as a whole, there are many pain receptors. There are fewer touch receptors, far fewer heat receptors, and fewest cold receptors.

toy

A toy is an object that people play with. Dolls, spinning tops, balls, and pull toys are among the earliest known toys. Children in ancient Egypt played with them at least 4,000 years ago. Kites were flown by Chinese children thousands of years ago. These toys and many others are still very popular.

Some toys are big enough to ride in, and others are small enough to fit in a pocket. The coal wagon at left was some child's treasured toy in the early 1900s.

Most of your toys probably came from toy stores or department stores. You may also have toys made especially for you by a relative or friend. Many children create their own toys, too. With a little imagination, toys can be made from simple objects and materials found around the house, yard, and garage. A piece of clay can be shaped into an animal or a spaceship. A cardboard box can be turned into a dollhouse or a car. String, buttons, fabric, paper, glue, wheels, lumber, and paint can all be used to make homemade toys.

Toys for Different Ages A baby's toys are simple and colorful. Rattles and stuffed animals are two favorite baby toys. Babies are also delighted by floating bath toys and by colorful *mobiles.* A mobile is a sort of hanger with brightly colored, movable shapes. It is hung above the crib, out of the baby's reach. Mobiles often have a small music box. When the music box is wound up, it plays a song. The baby can watch the moving shapes and listen to the song.

Toys for preschool children are designed to be fun and educational. For example, puzzles and blocks teach young children how to put things together and take them apart. Toys that "talk" help children learn numbers and words. Musical toys teach rhythm, melody, and harmony. (*See* **puzzle.**)

School-age children play with toys related to their own interests. Some collect toy trucks. Others play with dolls and puppets. Still other children like to paint or draw.

People never really outgrow their interest in toys. Many adults make collecting or building toys their hobbies. Dollhouses, dolls, and model trains, cars, airplanes, and ships are among the toys people build or collect—and sometimes still play with.

About $5 billion worth of toys are sold in the United States each year. But not all toys have been found to be safe. The U.S. government and private groups have been working to set safety standards for toys and to warn people about unsafe toys.

See also **hobby; doll;** and **puppet.**

Two track events—hurdles (left) and a relay race (right). Other track events include short races called dashes and distance races of a mile or more.

track and field

Track-and-field sports test the basic skills of men and women athletes. *Track events* are footraces of various lengths, and *field events* are throwing and jumping contests. Track-and-field events were held during the Olympic Games in ancient Greece, almost 3,000 years ago. Many of these events have changed little over the years and are still part of the Olympics.

Track-and-field events are held indoors or outdoors. Over 100 countries hold track and field meets, with athletes competing on local, national, and international levels. Runners race on an oval track. The distance around the track is called a *lap.* A lap around an outdoor track is ¼ mile (400 meters). Outdoor tracks are 24 feet (7.32 meters) wide and are divided into six to eight lanes. Indoor tracks are often smaller than outdoor tracks. Field events are held in the area inside the track.

Track Events The shortest track races are called *sprints.* Sprint races are under 440 yards and take only seconds to complete. *Middle-distance races* are between 440 yards and 1 mile (1,500 meters). *Long-distance races* are over 1 mile in length. In addition to speed, middle-distance and long-distance runners need *endurance*—the ability to keep up their strength for a

long time. *Relay races* are run by teams of four athletes each.

Hurdle races combine running and jumping skills. A hurdle is a fencelike object. Usually, ten hurdles are placed at regular spaces across the runner's lane. The height of the hurdles is different for men and women. The highest hurdles are 42 inches (106 centimeters) high. Skillful hurdlers lose little speed as they take long steps over the hurdles. The *steeplechase* is a long-distance race in which runners jump over hurdles and pits of water 12 feet (3.66 meters) square. *Walking races* are long-distance races in which athletes walk in a special way.

Field Events Jumping events include the *high jump, pole vault, long jump,* and *triple jump.* In the high jump and the pole vault, athletes jump over a bar that rests on two posts. If a jumper clears the bar, the bar is raised. A pole-vaulter carries a long, flexible pole and runs with it a short distance before jumping. When the bottom tip of the pole is almost under the raised bar, the athlete jams the pole into the ground. The pole bends, then straightens, and lifts the athlete. The pole-vaulter releases the pole and drops over the other side of the bar. For the long jump, athletes run down a short track and leap off the takeoff board at the end. In the triple jump, an athlete runs down the short

Field events—the pole vault (left), the long jump (right), and the javelin throw (below). Other field events include the high jump, the discus throw, and the shot put.

track until he reaches a white line. Then he hops and lands on the same foot, hops and lands on the other foot, hops on the first foot, and lands on one or two feet.

The four throwing events are the *discus, shot put, javelin,* and *hammer throw.* The discus is a flat object that looks like a dinner plate. The shot is a heavy lead ball that weighs up to 32 pounds (14 kilograms). The javelin is a spear that is 7 to 8 feet (2.1 to 2.4 meters) long. The hammer is a metal ball attached to a handle by steel wire—all together weighing 16 pounds (7.26 kilograms). Each of these four objects is thrown in a certain way to make it go as far as possible.

Special two-day events test the all-around ability of track-and-field athletes. The *pentathlon* is a series of five events. The *heptathlon* has seven events, and the *decathlon* has ten events.

Great Performances There have been many great track-and-field athletes. One of the best ever was Jesse Owens, who won four gold medals in track at the 1936 Olympics. At the 1968 Olympics, Bob Beamon of the United States won a gold medal in the long jump. He jumped 29 feet, 2½ inches (8.9 meters). Many people think that Beamon's jump is the greatest ever made. (*See* **Owens, Jesse.**)

See also **marathon.**

tragedy

In *Macbeth,* a play by William Shakespeare, a nobleman named Macbeth is told by three witches that he will be king. Macbeth wants to be king so much that he and his wife murder the king. The king's sons flee, and Macbeth becomes king, just as the witches had predicted. But after the murder, life for Macbeth is miserable. In the end, he loses his kingdom, his wife kills herself, and he is killed.

Macbeth is a tragedy. It is a serious play that ends unhappily for the main characters. Like other tragedies, *Macbeth* explores how people live and act. Macbeth and his wife are ambitious—eager to be powerful. We understand them, because we would like to be powerful, too. When ambition causes them to commit murder, they suffer for their crimes. Not only do others seek to punish them, but they cannot be at peace with themselves. We feel their misery. In some way, the story helps us understand and deal with our own ambitions.

The first writers of tragedy were the ancient Greeks. Their stories were about the kings and queens of the Greek city-states. The greatest tragedies in English are those of Shakespeare. Modern dramatists have written tragedies about common people.

See also **actors and acting; comedy;** and **melodrama.**

transistor, *see* electronics

transplant

Sometimes a body organ or some body tissue becomes so damaged or diseased that it cannot be repaired. In some cases, the organ or tissue can be replaced. The transfer of an organ or tissue from one part of the body to another, or from one person to another, is called a transplant. Transplants can help restore the health of people who might otherwise die or become disabled.

About 25 human organs and tissues can now be transplanted. Over 5,000 kidneys are transplanted each year. The lungs, heart, liver, and pancreas are other organs that can be transplanted. Surgeons have been transplanting heart valves, bone marrow, and cartilage for the last 20 years. Transplants of eye corneas have restored the sight of many people. Skin grafts—the transfer of skin from one part of the body to another—are used to repair damage from severe burns.

Transplants of organs or tissue from one person to another are not always successful. The body's immune system attacks and kills any foreign living cells. It protects the body against invading disease germs and foreign proteins. In the case of transplants, the immune system recognizes the transplant's proteins as foreign. It tries to *reject*—get rid of—the transplanted tissue or organ.

This equipment preserves human organs while surgeons prepare to transplant them.

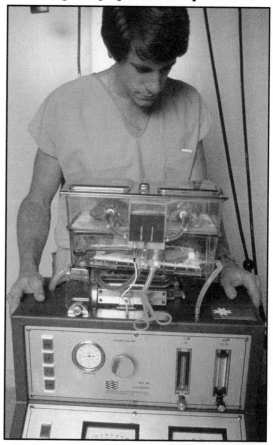

Left, transportation means moving goods—including compressed gas in huge tanks.
Right, transportation also means moving people. This pedicab driver uses his own power.

Transplants between blood relatives have the best chance of success. The body cells of relatives are more alike, so the patient's immune system is less likely to reject the transplant. Drugs can also be used to turn off the body's immune system. This prevents the transplanted tissue or organ from being rejected. But at the same time, these drugs weaken the body's chief means of fighting against disease and infection. The transplant patient can then easily become ill or infected. Recently, new drugs have been developed that prevent the immune system from rejecting transplants without destroying its ability to fight disease germs. As a result, transplants have become more successful.

transportation

Transportation is the moving of people and goods from one place to another. Cars, buses, and trucks carry people and cargo over roads and highways. In some areas of the world, goods are loaded onto pack animals. Railroads are another way to travel over land. Pipelines—aboveground and underground—carry water, oil, and natural gas long distances. Ferries, barges, and ships carry people and goods on rivers, lakes, canals, and oceans. Balloons, planes, and rockets are means of air travel.

We depend on transportation for many everyday things. For example, fresh milk goes from a dairy farm to a bottling plant in big tank trucks. The bottled milk travels to the city in delivery trucks. In the United States, fruits and vegetables grown in California are shipped in refrigerated railcars to the rest of the nation. In winter, fresh fruit is flown in from Mexico, Central America, Australia, and Israel. Your clothing may have been sewn in Sri Lanka, Malaysia, or Hong Kong and shipped to your city. Your family car may have been shipped by freighter from Japan, Korea, Mexico, or Europe.

Industry depends on transportation to bring raw materials to factories, plants, and mills. A steel mill, for example, needs tons of iron ore from an iron mine. It also needs tons of coal to provide the heat to process the metal. These materials come by ship, train, rail, or truck.

We also depend on transportation for personal travel. You probably use some form of transportation every day to go to and from school and visit friends. You may travel by bicycle, bus, or car. In an hour, a car can carry you a distance that would take you all day to walk.

In 1850, the trip from New York City to San Francisco took several months. You could sail around South America, or ride a horse or wagon overland along rugged trails. The trip was not only slow, but also dangerous. Many travelers who started out died from hardships along the way. Today, you can travel between these two cities in about five hours by plane, or in about three days and nights by train or bus. Business people and government officials think nothing of boarding a plane to attend a meeting in another country.

Modern transportation has enabled us to save lives in medical emergencies and natural disasters. If a patient needs a rare type of blood, the doctor may have it flown in from a blood bank in another city or state. Helicopters fly teams of medical workers to the scene of a fire or serious accident. The helicopters can fly injured people to the hospital while the medical team begins treatment. Planes and helicopters also speed fire fighters to remote forest fires.

In Wartime Transportation has changed the ways we fight wars, too. Armies used to fight on foot or on horseback. But during World War II, Germany used *blitzkrieg* —"lightning war." During a blitzkrieg, planes attacked from the air, while ground forces attacked with motorized vehicles, such as tanks. The invention of the submarine and helicopter also changed warfare. Today, ballistic missiles make instant attacks possible. (*See* **missile; submarine; aircraft; tank;** and **helicopter.**)

Planning Around Transportation Transportation systems have changed the shape of the land. We have dug canals to link rivers, lakes, and seas. We have leveled the earth to make smooth beds for rail lines and highways. We have bored tunnels through mountains and built bridges across canyons and ravines. (*See* **bridge; canal; highway; subway;** and **tunnel.**)

Cities have grown up along trade routes, and around harbors and ports. Suburbs have grown up along highways and rail lines. These routes allow people to travel to and from jobs in the cities. (*See* **harbors and ports** and **suburb.**)

Huge airports have been built near big cities. New roads have been built for getting cargo and people to and from the airports. Hundred of planes fly into and out of major airports each day.

The world's countless air, land, and water routes overlap. This makes it possible to travel and to trade goods around the world,

TIMELINE OF TRANSPORTATION

Ancient Times

1600s

and to reach remote villages and farms. Manufacturing and trade as we know it today would not be possible without our complex transportation network.

History Early peoples traveled by foot and by rafts. They carried loads on *sledges* —small wooden platforms or boxes that were pulled over the ground or snow on runners. Heavy objects could be rolled on logs or floated on rafts.

In the Middle East around 3200 B.C., oxen were trained to pull loads. When the wheel was invented—around 3000 B.C.—people built wooden carts and wagons and hitched the oxen to them. Later, camels, goats, and horses were put to work pulling wagons or carrying riders or packs.

In the Americas, the llama was used as a pack animal and dogs were used to drag sledges. There is some evidence that American peoples knew about the wheel, but it was not used for transportation. This may have been because people and pack animals could move along narrow, rocky trails, but wheeled vehicles need wide, cleared roads. The Persians and Romans built highways across their empires in order to move their armies easily. In South America, the Inca built a highway system over the Andes Mountains as a way to carry messages and goods to the capital.

Land transportation became speedier with the development of engines. The first steam locomotive rolled on rails in 1804. By the middle 1800s, railroads crossed the United States from north to south and from east to west. Before this, heavy cargoes were sent only by water. (*See* **railroad.**)

Steam was also used to power the first automobiles and trucks. In the 1880s, the new gasoline engine was added to a car. Since then, most cars and small trucks have been powered by gasoline engines. (*See* **automobile** and **trucks and trucking.**)

The sail was invented at about the same time as the wheel. Sails made it easier and faster to travel on rivers and to cross large lakes. People even began to cross the seas and settle in new lands.

Engines were also added to boats and ships. The steam engine powered a boat for the first time in 1798. Boats no longer had to rely on variable winds for their speed. Boats and ships are also powered by gasoline motors, and some submarines are even powered by nuclear reactors. (*See* **ship.**)

1800s

1900s

Balloons provided the first form of air travel, but they never became very important in transportation. The first airplane took off in 1903. The jet engine was invented in the 1930s and was used to propel speedy jets. Today, airplanes and jets are our most important means of traveling quickly over a long distance. (*See* **balloon** and **jet engine.**)

Space transportation is still at an early stage. People have orbited Earth, and gone to the moon and to orbiting space stations. With future space stations, there will be more transportation of people through space. Someday, we may bring natural resources, such as metal ores, back from space to be used in manufacturing. We may also manufacture goods in space and then bring them to Earth. (*See* **space exploration** and **space station.**)

tree

A tree is a green plant with a woody trunk. Trees grow for many years. Some trees are the largest plants and the oldest living things on Earth.

Most trees have branches. These give a tree its shape and lift the leaves to the sunlight. Some trees—such as spruces and firs—are shaped like cones. Their lowest and longest branches are near the ground. As you look up the trunk, the branches become shorter. Other trees—such as maples and elms—lose the branches closest to the ground. Their branches begin higher on the trunk and give the tree a lollipop shape. Most palm trees have no branches. Their large leaves come out of the top of the trunk. As the trunk grows taller, the leaves are lifted higher.

Parts of Trees Trees have three main parts—roots, trunk (including the tree's branches), and leaves. Trees also have flowers, fruit, nuts, seed pods, or cones.

The root system can be very large. Some root systems grow as deep as the tree is tall. Many trees have roots that spread 6 or more meters (20 feet) out from the tree. The roots

anchor the tree in the soil and collect the water and minerals the plant needs to grow. The roots also store food for the tree. (*See* **roots.**)

A tree's trunk, branches, and roots are covered with a tough *outer bark* made of hard, dead cells. The outer bark protects the tree from the weather and from insects. The *inner bark* is softer. Food made in the leaves flows down the inner bark to the roots. Under the bark is a thin layer of cells called the *cambium.* The cells of the cambium divide and make the trunk, branches, and roots grow thicker. A tree grows taller when a bud develops into a *twig*—a young branch. As the branch grows, it produces more and more buds.

Most of the inside of the trunk and branches is *wood.* The wood has two layers. The *heartwood* runs through the center of the trunk and branches. It is formed by the tough cell walls of thousands of dead cells. Surrounding it is the live *sapwood,* which is full of tiny pipelines. The *sap*—mineral-rich water—flows up the sapwood.

Three important kinds of trees. Palms grow in warm climates. Broadleafs grow in moderate climates. Evergreens grow even in regions that are very cold or very dry.

evergreen

broadleaf

palm

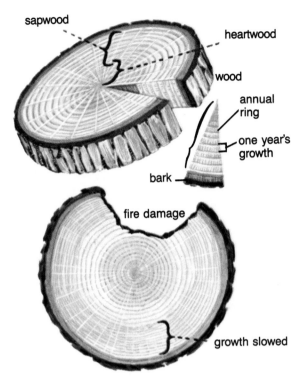

sapwood

heartwood

wood

annual ring

one year's growth

bark

fire damage

growth slowed

When a tree is cut down, the wood reveals many things about the tree's life.

If you look at a cut tree trunk, you will see that the wood is made up of rings, one inside the other. Some rings are light-colored and others are dark. These rings show how the tree grows. The light rings are called *spring-wood* or *earlywood*. They show the fast growth during the spring. The dark rings are *summerwood* or *latewood*. They show the slower growth during summer. Together, a light ring and a dark ring show a single year's growth and are called an *annual ring*. You can count annual rings to find out how old a tree is.

Some annual rings are thicker than others. Thick annual rings form when there is a lot of rainfall. Thin annual rings form when rainfall is scarce. Scientists use annual rings to learn about weather in the past. Three kinds of trees in California are especially helpful for this purpose. Some coastal redwoods are more than 2,000 years old. Some giant sequoias are more than 3,000 years old. Some bristlecone pines are over 4,000 years old. (*See* **dates and dating.**)

Leaves grow at the tips of twigs. The leaves are where *photosynthesis* is carried out. In this process, plants use the sun's energy to make sugar and oxygen from water and carbon dioxide. The tree uses the sugar for food. It releases the oxygen into the air. (*See* **photosynthesis.**)

Kinds of Trees Trees can be grouped in different ways. One way is based on how long they keep their leaves. *Evergreen* trees keep their leaves all year. They lose a few leaves at a time, but there are always leaves on the tree. *Broadleaf* trees lose all of their leaves each autumn and grow new leaves the next spring.

Trees can also be grouped by how they make seeds. Some trees make their seeds in cones. The cone-bearing trees include pines, cedars, and many other evergreens. Other trees—such as dogwood, aspen, and oaks—are flowering plants. They make their seeds in flowers. (*See* **seed; cone-bearing plant; evergreen tree;** and **flowering plant.**)

Trees grow over much of the world. They grow best where the soil is fairly deep. Evergreen trees can live in poor, rocky soil. Broadleaf trees grow better in rich soil. Trees grow best in areas that receive at least 50 centimeters (20 inches) of rain and snow a year. It is also important that moisture be available during the spring and summer growing seasons. Trees do not grow in the driest deserts, because there is so little rainfall. Few trees grow in grasslands, which often have *droughts*—months without rain. Trees do not grow above the *timberline*—the height on mountains above which there is not enough moisture and air for the trees to survive. (*See* **grassland** and **timberline.**)

Broadleaf trees are most common in places that receive more than 75 centimeters (30 inches) of rain each year. Evergreen trees grow widely in areas that receive 38 to 100 centimeters (15 to 40 inches) of rain and snow. They do well in drier areas because their leaves are shaped like needles or scales and are covered with wax. These leaves lose little water. The large, flat leaves of broadleaf trees lose a lot of water.

Uses of Trees Trees provide homes and food for many living things. Squirrels and

Many birds make their nests in trees and eat the insects living in tree bark or among tree leaves. Other animals use trees for shelter or food, too.

birds live among their branches. Mice, rabbits, and chipmunks build dens among their roots. Insects and worms burrow under their bark to live and feed. Beavers build their dams and lodges with tree branches. Many animals eat the fruits, nuts, seeds, and buds of trees.

People depend on trees, too. We cut the wood of trees into lumber for building houses, furniture, and other things. We also grind the the wood into pulp for making paper and cardboard. (*See* **wood** and **paper.**)

We use the sap produced by certain trees. The sap of the sugar maple is made into syrup, sugar, and candy. Rubber trees produce sap that contains *latex*—an elastic material used in paints and many other products. Turpentine, a paint thinner, comes from the sap of pine trees that grow in the southeastern United States. (*See* **maple syrup** and **rubber.**)

Certain medicines come from trees. Quinine, from the cinchona tree of South America, is used to treat fevers caused by malaria and other diseases. Willow trees are a natural source of the painkiller used in aspirin.

We eat the fruits of some flowering trees. We grow these trees in orchards and harvest the apples, cherries, pears, oranges, dates, and many other fruits they produce. We also grow some trees for their nuts. Pecans, walnuts, and filberts are some of the nuts we enjoy. (*See* **apple; citrus fruit;** and **nut.**)

We plant other trees for their flowers. Magnolias, dogwoods, and flowering quinces have beautiful flowers. We enjoy trees for their shapes and for the beautiful colors of their leaves. We plant some trees because they give shade or form a living fence. Russian olive and lombardy poplar are two trees used to make living fences. They quickly grow tall enough to block ugly sights and noise.

See also **forest; forestry; hardwood tree; jungle; leaf; pine; rain forest; redwoods and sequoias;** and **biome.**

Trinidad and Tobago, *see* West Indies

Trojan War

The Trojan War was a conflict between ancient Greece and the city of Troy. It lasted ten years and probably took place from 1184 to

1193 B.C. The war and its heroes inspired plays, poems, and sculpture. Most of what we know about the war comes from the *Iliad,* an epic poem by Homer, a great Greek storyteller. The fall of Troy is described in the *Aeneid,* by the Roman poet Virgil. (*See* **Homer.**)

No one is sure what events led to the war. According to legend, the war had its beginning when the goddess Eris, a troublemaker, sent a golden apple to a party of the gods. The apple was for the most beautiful goddess. Hera, Athena, and Aphrodite each claimed that the apple was meant for her. They asked Paris, a Trojan prince, to decide who deserved the apple.

Each of the goddesses tempted Paris to name herself as the fairest. Hera promised him great riches. Athena promised him success in war. He chose Aphrodite, who promised to give him Helen, the most beautiful woman in the world.

Helen was already the wife of King Menelaus of Sparta, a Greek city-state. But she went with Paris back to Troy. The Greeks swore to punish Troy and to get Helen back.

King Agamemnon of Mycenae, another Greek city-state, led the Greek army against Troy. Menelaus and the heroes Odysseus, Achilles, Ajax, and Nestor fought with the Greeks. King Priam and his sons Hector and Paris led the Trojans. The war went on for years. The high, thick walls around Troy were impossible for the Greeks to break down. On the battlefield, both armies fought with all their strength.

In the tenth year of the war, Odysseus ordered his men to build a huge wooden horse. The horse was hollow, and some Greek soldiers hid inside it. The Greeks left the horse outside the city walls, then boarded their ships and pretended to sail away.

The curious Trojans took the horse into their city. That night, the Greek soldiers hidden in the horse sneaked out and opened the city gates. The rest of the Greek army quickly poured in. The Greeks killed most of the Trojans and burned Troy. Helen was returned to Menelaus.

Greek historians believed that the Trojan War really happened. But for hundreds of years, many people thought it was only a legend. In the late 1800s, archaeologists uncovered the ruins of ancient Troy. The things they found at Troy—and writings found at other ancient cities—showed that the Greek historians were correct.

See also **Troy.**

The Trojans took a huge horse left by the Greek army into their city. At night, Greek soldiers climbed out of the hollow horse and opened the city gates to the Greek army.

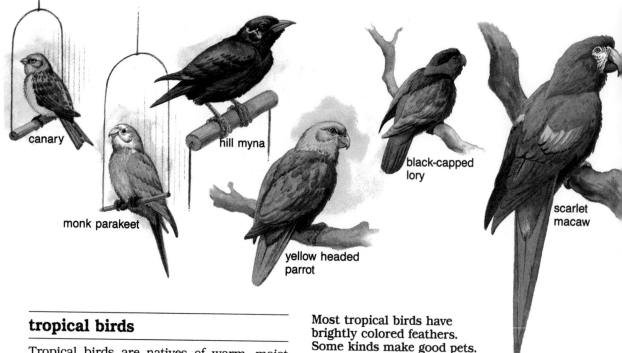

canary

monk parakeet

hill myna

yellow headed parrot

black-capped lory

scarlet macaw

tropical birds

Tropical birds are natives of warm, moist lands. Most have bright feathers and live in forests. You can see many tropical birds in zoos. A few kinds are kept as pets.

Canaries Canaries are small members of the finch family. They are named for the Canary Islands off the northwest coast of Africa. A wild canary has olive green feathers with gray steaks and a yellow underbelly. Europeans started to tame and breed the birds as early as the 1300s. Canaries are still popular pets, prized for their singing. Canaries should be fed small seeds and some green leaves. They also need the mineral lime. You can supply this by attaching a cuttlefish bone to the cage.

Mynahs These members of the starling family come from India, Burma, and other parts of Asia. They eat mainly fruit. The well-known *talking mynah* is a medium-size bird with black or dark feathers, an orange streak on each wing, an orange beak, and yellow feet. This noisy bird can learn to say words and phrases.

The Parrot Family This family includes parrots, cockatoos, lovebirds, lorikeets, parakeets, and macaws. These birds have sharp, hooked bills.

Many parrots can be taught to imitate the sounds people make when they are talking. The best "talkers" are the African gray parrot and the green Amazon parrot.

Most tropical birds have brightly colored feathers. Some kinds make good pets.

Many cockatoos are mostly white with yellow or pink markings. Some are black or gray. The cockatoo has a tuft on its head that opens like a fan. These beautiful birds come from Australia and some Pacific Islands.

Lovebirds are small parrots that like to cuddle. They are happiest when kept in pairs. They usually have green feathers, but the face may be a different color. They eat seeds and fruit.

Lorikeets—"lories"—are small and brilliantly colored. The rainbow lorikeet has a blue head, red chest and bill, and green back and wings, with yellow and red markings under their wings. Lories eat nectar, fruit, and insects.

Parakeets are small parrots that live in the Americas, Australia, Tasmania, Africa, India, and Southeast Asia. The Carolina parakeet used to live in the United States. Most parakeets have a combination of two or three of these colors—green, blue, violet, yellow, white, and gray. Parakeets eat seeds. The most popular parakeet is the budgerigar—"budgie." It can learn words. It loves to climb and swing, so its cage should have a ladder, swing, and perch.

Macaws are the largest parrots. Including the tail, their bodies may be 90 centimeters (3 feet) long. These noisy birds have brilliant feathers of red, blue, and green. Macaws use

toco
toucan

their powerful beaks to crack seeds and nuts. If the bird is frightened or mistreated, it will snap with its beak. Many people keep a macaw tied to a perch instead of in a cage.

Toucans Toucans live in the rain forests of Central and South America. They have large, brightly colored bills. They eat fruit and travel in flocks. Toucans are not often kept as pets, because they are very difficult to care for.

Birds of Paradise These birds live in northern Australia, New Guinea, and the nearby islands. Feathers with unusual forms and colors droop from the head and tail. Some feathers even end in curls. The males can raise and display their tail and head feathers. These birds are protected—it is illegal to hunt them.

Caring for Pet Birds Tropical birds must never be exposed to cold or drafts. Place the cage where the bird will get fresh air, and both light and shade. Do not put it in direct sunlight, or the bird will get so hot that it will faint or die.

Each kind of bird has its own diet. Check a book or ask a pet-store owner what is the best diet for your bird. Give your pet fresh water every day.

The bird's home should be sturdy and large enough for the bird to fly freely without hitting its wings. It should have perches of various sizes, some near the bottom and others up higher. Clean the cage and the perches every day. Also clean the food and water containers. This will help keep your bird from getting sick.

Birds need exercise. Flying around a room in your home should be part of your bird's regular routine. Before letting the bird out, close all windows and doors. Cover windows and mirrors so the bird will not fly into them. Keep cats and dogs out. While the bird is free, keep the cage door open so the bird can return when it is ready.

Birds need darkness for sleeping, so cover the cage with a light cloth at night.

Birds like attention. Spend some time each day playing with your bird. You may want to teach it tricks or to speak, too.

tropical fish

Tropical fish are popular pets. People enjoy watching and raising these colorful small fish in home aquariums.

Several hundred kinds of tropical fish are sold in stores. If you know a little about the different kinds, you will be able to choose what is best for your collection.

Guppies, mollies, and tetras are tropical fish often raised in home fish tanks.

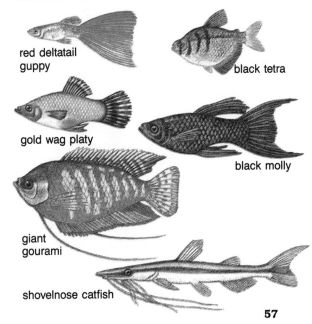

red deltatail guppy

black tetra

gold wag platy

black molly

giant gourami

shovelnose catfish

57

Most tropical fish are from the tropics—regions near the equator—where the water is warm. Others, despite the name, are from cooler waters. To keep tropical fish healthy, the water in their aquarium should be like the water in their native home.

Freshwater fish are easier to raise than saltwater fish. So for your first aquarium, begin with freshwater fish, such as guppies and platies. As you become more experienced, you can add different kinds of fish to the aquarium. But you cannot add saltwater fish to a freshwater aquarium.

Do not put too many fish in an aquarium. Most of the fish sold in stores are young. They will grow after you buy them. If an aquarium gets too crowded, the fish will become upset and may begin to fight.

If you plan to have several kinds in one aquarium, choose fish that get along with each other. Some, such as cichlids, are *carnivores*—meat-eaters. You would not want them in an aquarium with smaller fish.

You need to know what foods your fish eat. Feed your fish small amounts several times a day rather than one big meal once a day. Give them only as much food as they will eat in one or two minutes. Leftover food can pollute the water and cause the fish to have health problems.

Some fish feed at the surface. Others feed in midwater. Still others, such as catfish, are bottom feeders. A well-stocked aquarium will include fish of each type. Working together, the different fish will help keep the aquarium clean.

Breeding fish can be exciting. Some fish, such as guppies and mollies, are *live-bearers.* Their young develop inside the mother's body. Other fish, such as gouramis and tetras, are *egg-layers.* Sometimes the babies must be separated from adult fish. Baby fish need different foods than adults. You can learn more about breeding fish from pet shops and guidebooks.

See also **aquarium** and **sea horse.**

tropics

The tropics are geographical regions that form a broad belt around the middle of the earth. These regions are centered around the equator. They contain most of the earth's warmest and dampest places.

The outer boundaries of the tropics are the Tropic of Cancer, 1,600 miles (2,560

The tropics are the regions between the Tropic of Cancer and the Tropic of Capricorn. The land regions in light green have tropical rain forests.

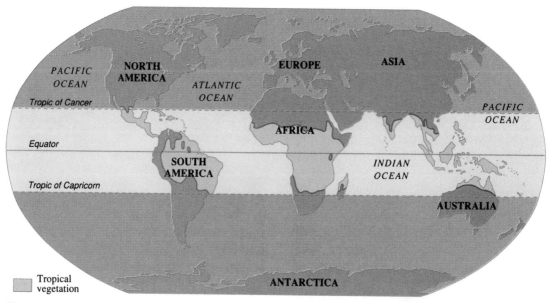

Tropical vegetation

kilometers) north of the equator, and the Tropic of Capricorn, 1,600 miles (2,560 kilometers) south of the equator. On the first day of summer in the Northern Hemisphere (around June 21), the sun is directly above the Tropic of Cancer. On the first day of winter in the Northern Hemisphere (around December 21), the sun is directly above the Tropic of Capricorn.

In the tropics, there are only small differences in the times of sunrise and sunset. Day and night are always about the same length. The tropics are warm because the sun shines directly on them all year.

Though all tropic regions have warm temperatures (except at high altitudes), they have different climates. Places with a lot of rainfall have tropical rain forests. Places with a short rainy season and a longer dry season have grasslands called *savannas*. Some of the world's great deserts are in tropic regions. (*See* **rain forest; grassland;** and **desert.**)

About three-fourths of Africa, all of South Asia, and nearly half of Australia are in the tropics. The tropics cover the northern two-thirds of South America, all of Central America and the West Indies, and the southern half of Mexico. The only tropical part of the United States is Hawaii.

Troy

Troy was an ancient Asian city located in the region that is now Turkey. It was made famous by Greek legend and by Homer's long poem the *Iliad.* The poem is about a war fought near the city by the Greeks and the people of Troy, called Trojans. (*See* **Homer.**)

For centuries, people thought the Trojan War was just a legend. But in the late 1800s, a German businessman named Heinrich Schliemann came to believe otherwise. He had spent years studying the *Iliad.* Based on his reading, he decided that a hill near the town of Hissarlik in Turkey was the site of ancient Troy. In 1870, he began to dig there. After 20 years of work, he uncovered the

The war described by Homer may have been fought near these ruins of ancient Troy.

ruins of several ancient cities. He believed that one of them was Troy.

Schliemann's assistant, Wilhelm Dorpfeld, continued digging at the site. During the 1890s, he identified nine cities, built one on top of the other. The oldest city was built around 3000 B.C. Each city was protected by thick stone walls and towers. The second and sixth cities were wealthy. Most experts believe that the seventh city was the one involved in the Trojan War. It was built sometime after 1300 B.C., and was looted and burned by a Greek army around 1250 B.C.

See also **Trojan War.**

trucks and trucking

Trucks are vehicles that carry goods over roads and highways. Trucks are built in a range of sizes and for a variety of purposes. Like cars, they are usually powered by a gasoline or diesel engine.

Before there were trucks, goods were carried on carts and wagons pulled by horses, oxen, mules, or dogs. The first trucks appeared around 1900. They were just cars that people had changed so large objects would fit in them. They might have removed the back seat or trunk and have laid down a floor. These trucks held little more than a family station wagon does today.

Factories first began building trucks in 1910. That year, 5,000 trucks were manufactured in the United States. Today, U.S. factories manufacture more than a million new trucks of all types and sizes each year. Many more trucks are manufactured by foreign makers.

Types of Trucks Some trucks are built for specific jobs. A tank truck is designed to transport liquids, such as milk or oil. Refrigerated dairy trucks, cement-mixing trucks, fire trucks, and garbage trucks are other kinds of specialized trucks. Most trucks are designed to transport a variety of goods. Trucks may be divided into several basic categories, depending on their weight, size, and power.

Light trucks, such as vans and pickup trucks, have a *gross weight* of less than 6,000 kilograms (14,000 pounds). Gross weight is the weight of the truck plus its cargo. Light trucks are also called *single-unit* or *straight* trucks, because they are built on a single frame.

Medium trucks have a gross weight of up to 12,000 kilograms (26,000 pounds). They are bigger and more powerful than light trucks, with much heavier frames, axles, suspensions, and wheels. Often, they have double sets of rear wheels. Medium trucks are also single-unit trucks. Light and medium trucks are used to carry light cargoes distances less than about 640 kilometers (400 miles).

Heavy trucks are used for carrying heavy cargoes for long distances. There are two main types of heavy trucks—*heavy straight trucks* and *tractor trailers.* A heavy straight truck has a gross weight of more than 12,000 kilograms (26,000 pounds) and is

KINDS OF TRUCKS

18-wheeler (milk truck)

ready-mix cement truck

delivery van

built on a single frame. Many can carry cargo that weighs twice as much as the truck.

Tractor trailers are sometimes called *combination trucks.* This is because they have two separate parts—the tractor and the trailer. The tractor must contain a very powerful engine, because it has to pull the large, heavy trailer that is attached to it. The tractor section is sometimes called the *cab,* because the driver and sometimes a passenger sit in it.

Many medium and heavy trucks today are *flatbed trucks.* The cargo section is a flat platform designed to transport *containerized* cargo. Goods that are containerized do not have to be lifted box by box from a train, ship, or truck. Instead, the goods are in a large container, and just the container needs to be lifted.

Trucks can be grouped by how many axles and wheels they have. The milk truck at left has 5 axles and 18 wheels. The lightweight pickup has 2 axles and 4 wheels.

pickup truck

fuel truck

Trucking Almost everything that is transported makes at least part of the trip by truck. Trucks are the link between all other kinds of freight transport. They can go wherever there is a road, while trains can go only where there are rail lines, and ships can sail only in deep water. Many goods make their entire trip by truck, especially over distances of a few hundred miles or less. Most cities, for example, get their milk delivered by truck from dairies near the cities.

Transporting goods over longer distances usually involves a combination of trucking and some other means of travel. Suppose, for example, an automobile factory in Detroit is sending a shipment of new cars to dealers in Florida. The shipment travels most of the way by railroad. When the train reaches Florida, the cars are unloaded onto trucks. The trucks drive to the dealers around the state. Sometimes, a loaded truck is carried partway to its destination by railroad and then driven the rest of the way. Carrying the already-loaded truck in a railroad car is called *piggybacking.*

Truman, Harry S.

Harry S. Truman was the 33rd president of the United States. He held office from 1945 to 1953.

Truman was born in Lamar, Missouri, in 1884. When he was six, his family moved to Independence, Missouri. Harry wanted to attend the United States Military Academy at West Point. But he had poor eyesight, and the academy did not accept him. Instead, he held several jobs and ran the family farm.

In 1917, the United States entered World War I. Truman fought in France and rose to captain. In 1919, he married Bess Wallace. Later that year, he opened a clothing store in Kansas City. But the store failed, and Truman decided to try a career in politics. In 1922, he was elected as a county commissioner, and in 1926, as a presiding judge on the county court. He was elected to the U.S. Senate in 1934 and reelected in 1940.

Truman was president from 1945 to 1953. He led the U.S. during difficult times.

In 1941, the United States entered World War II. Truman was named chairman of a Senate committee investigating waste in military spending. The committee saved the nation millions of dollars and brought Truman national fame. The Democratic party chose him as their candidate for vice president in 1944. He ran with presidential candidate Franklin D. Roosevelt. Roosevelt and Truman won the election.

In April 1945, President Roosevelt died, and Truman became president. He faced many problems. World War II was still going on. Germany surrendered in early May, but Japan continued to fight. In early August 1945, Truman ordered the dropping of atomic bombs on two Japanese cities. On September 2, Japan surrendered, and World War II was over. (*See* **Hiroshima**.)

After World War II, several European countries came under the control of the Soviet Union. Truman felt the United States could stop the spread of Soviet power by giving aid to noncommunist countries. This policy became known as the Truman Doctrine. Congress approved the Marshall Plan in 1947. Through the Marshall Plan, the United States lent money to European nations to help them rebuild their countries.

Few people thought Truman could win the 1948 presidential election. But he traveled all over the nation, making speeches, and won over the voters. During his second term, the United States formed a mutual defense pact—the North Atlantic Treaty Organization (NATO)—with Canada, Britain, France, Italy, and other European countries. NATO is still very important to U.S. foreign policy. In 1950, Truman sent American troops to help South Korea fight communist North Korea. The nation was still involved in the Korean War when Truman left office in 1953. He retired to Missouri, where he died in 1972.

Truth, Sojourner

Sojourner Truth was a black American woman who worked to end slavery and to bring about equal rights for women.

Sojourner Truth was born a slave in Ulster County, New York, around 1797. She was named Isabella Baumfree. As a young woman, she ran away when her master broke his promise to free her. She became free in 1828, when New York passed a law making slavery illegal.

In 1843, Baumfree believed she heard the voice of God speaking to her. She said that he had commanded her to preach his message of love and justice throughout the world. After this experience, she changed her name to Sojourner Truth and began to travel through New England and the Midwest. Wherever she traveled, she made fiery speeches urging people to end slavery. She even visited the White House to speak to President Abraham Lincoln.

Following the Civil War (1861 to 1865), the 13th Amendment became part of the United States Constitution. This amendment outlawed slavery in the United States.

Sojourner Truth continued to speak out against the unfair treatment of women. Until her death in 1883, she worked hard for women's rights.

See also **slavery** and **women's rights**.

Tubman, Harriet

Harriet Tubman was a black American who helped many slaves escape to freedom. She was born a slave on a Maryland plantation around 1820. She first worked as a maid and a nurse. After she turned 12, she worked in the fields. In 1844, she married John Tubman, a freed slave.

One night in 1849, Tubman ran away. Following the North Star, she traveled to the North. She then became active in the Underground Railroad, a group of people who worked together to help slaves escape to Canada. (*See* **Underground Railroad.**)

Over the next 15 years, Tubman made 20 dangerous trips to the South and led out about 300 slaves—including her parents. It was against the law to help runaway slaves, and slave owners offered as much as $40,000 for Harriet Tubman's capture. But no one ever caught her. Tubman said, "I never ran my train off the track, and I never lost a passenger."

Harriet Tubman served as a spy, scout, and nurse for the Union army during the Civil War (1861 to 1865). After slavery was outlawed in 1865, she settled in Auburn, New York. She collected money for schools for blacks, and founded a home for elderly freed slaves. She died in 1913.

See also **slavery.**

Harriet Tubman helped more than 300 slaves escape from their owners.

tundra

The tundra is a biome found in lands around the North Pole—Greenland, Iceland, and the northern parts of Alaska, Canada, Scandinavia, Finland, and Russia. The biome near the tops of the world's highest mountains is also tundra. The tundra environment can be harsh. Winters in the northern tundra are very long and very cold. Snow falls, but it is dry and powdery. The tundra receives only 20 to 30 centimeters (8 to 12 inches) of moisture during a year. Strong winds blow all the time. Summer lasts less than two months. (*See* **biome.**)

The tundra is often rocky and bare. Soil forms slowly and is often very shallow. Dead plants and animals decay slowly in the cold temperatures. It takes a long time for the materials in their bodies to break down and become part of the soil. (*See* **soil.**)

In the northern tundra, the soil is called the *permafrost* because it is always frozen. Even in summer, only the top layer thaws, becoming spongy and filled with water.

The harsh conditions in the tundra make it impossible for trees to grow there. Tundra plants are mostly grasses, small shrubs, small leafy herbs, and a kind of lichen called *reindeer moss.* The climate and poor soil make the plants grow slowly, staying low to the ground and close together. They form a carpet that bursts into bloom during the short summer. For awhile, white, yellow, and blue flowers fill the tundra landscape. (*See* **grass** and **lichen.**)

In summer, the tundra's marshy top layer of soil is a perfect breeding place for insects. The plentiful insects are sources of food for many birds. Because food is so easily available, the tundra is also a breeding ground for many kinds of migratory birds. Arctic terns breed in the northern tundra, and then migrate all the way to the Antarctic—more than 13,000 kilometers (8,000 miles) away! Many kinds of ducks lay eggs and rear their young in the tundra. When summer ends, the ducks fly south to warmer climates.

Few large animals live in the tundra all year. In North America, musk oxen and caribou are year-round tundra residents. In northern Europe and Asia, reindeer are the tundra residents. These animals have thick, shaggy coats that keep them warm. They eat grasses and reindeer moss. In winter, they use their hooves to clear away the snow so they can get to the plants.

Arctic foxes, polar bears, and a variety of seals live along the tundra's ocean coasts. Polar bears and seals feed on ocean fish. Arctic foxes often follow polar bears and feed on the leftovers from their meals. The foxes also eat small mouselike animals called *lemmings.* The snowshoe hare and plump birds called *ptarmigans* are other small animals that live in the tundra.

The polar bear's white coat lets this large animal blend into the snow and ice. Most Arctic foxes have white fur during winter. In summer, the fur turns brown. Snowshoe hares and ptarmigans change their colors, too. In summer, they are brown and blend in with the shrubs. In winter, they grow new white fur or feathers to blend with the snow.

At the edge of the tundra, where the climate is less harsh, the tundra blends into the evergreen-forest biome. There is no clear line with tundra on one side and evergreen trees on the other. Instead, there is an area of dwarf trees called the *krummholz.* The word *krummholz* means "twisted wood," and that is just what the trees look like. The wind and cold make the trees grow small and twisted. Often, they cannot grow upright. Their trunks grow along the ground and only the branches reach up. The krummholz has an eerie appearance and is sometimes called the *elfin forest.*

Few people live in the tundra, because the climate is so harsh there. Some Eskimo live in parts of the tundra where they can fish and hunt.

tungsten

Tungsten is a whitish metal and an element. The *filament*—the thin metal wire—inside an incandescent light bulb is made of tungsten. When the bulb is lit, the filament glows. Tungsten is used as a filament because it has the highest melting point of any metal—3,410° C (6,106° F).

Even at very high temperatures, tungsten does not combine easily with oxygen. It

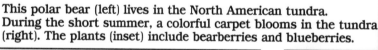

This polar bear (left) lives in the North American tundra. During the short summer, a colorful carpet blooms in the tundra (right). The plants (inset) include bearberries and blueberries.

Tunnels pass through the solid rock of a mountain. Without the tunnels, the road would have to wind up one side of the mountain and down the other.

resists corrosion—being weakened by other elements and compounds. Tungsten is often added to iron, aluminum, and other metals to make strong *alloys*—blends of metals. Alloys containing tungsten are used to make tools, knives, rocket nozzles, and missile and engine parts.

Tungsten is chemically combined with carbon to form tungsten carbide. This is a very hard and heat-resistant compound used to cut and form hot steel.

Tungsten is one of the heaviest elements. It is often used where both strength and weight are needed, such as in the wheel of a gyroscope. (*See* **gyroscope**.)

The United States, South Korea, Bolivia, the Soviet Union, Portugal, and Burma have large deposits of tungsten ores. Except in the United States, tungsten is known as *wolfram*. The chemical symbol for tungsten, W, stands for "wolfram."

Tunisia, *see* Africa

tunnel

A tunnel is an underground passageway. Tunnels provide routes for cars and trains through mountains, under rivers, or beneath city streets. Some tunnels are huge. Other tunnels are just large enough to fit underground pipes for carrying water, natural gas, or sewage.

History People first began building tunnels late in the Stone Age, thousands of years ago. They used picks made from antlers and bones to dig tunnels so that they could mine flint that was buried deep underground. They needed flint to make tools and weapons. Today, mines still have tunnels to reach underground deposits of gems, metals, and fossil fuels.

About 4,000 years ago, the Babylonians built the first major tunnel to be used for transportation. It was an underwater passage that linked the royal palace in the city of Babylon with a temple on the other side of the Euphrates River.

The ancient Romans constructed tunnels to carry water as part of their system of aqueducts. Their armies also dug tunnels under the walls of the cities they were attacking. Beneath Rome and other cities, early Christians created underground passageways called *catacombs*. The catacombs were burial sites and hiding places.

The modern era of tunnel building began in the 1700s with the construction of canal tunnels. These tunnels allowed water to flow through mountains.

In the 1800s, dynamite was invented, and compressed-air drills were developed. These led to an increase in tunnel building. Tunnels were blasted and drilled through mountains and under rivers. Railroads could be built anywhere. In major cities, subway tunnels were constructed. (*See* **subway.**)

Kinds of Tunnels   There are four kinds of tunnels—*rock tunnels, soft-earth tunnels, underwater tunnels,* and *cut-and-cover tunnels.* Two factors determine which kind of tunnel is dug at a particular site—the kind of ground through which the tunnel must go, and the depth of the tunnel.

Rock tunnels are cut through solid rock. Workers bore holes into the rock with steel drills or diamond-tipped drills. Then they pack dynamite into the holes and blast away a section of rock. After the smoke clears, they remove the rubble and repeat the process in the next section of rock. Sometimes the rock walls of a tunnel are so sturdy that they need no added support. More often, steel supports are used to prevent cave-ins. An inner layer of *reinforced concrete*—concrete with steel rods through it—keeps dirt, water, and loose stones from falling into the tunnel.

As tunnel workers dig deep underground, fresh air becomes scarce. Large fans pump outside air into the tunnel. The fans can be reversed to suck out the dust created by blasting.

The first great rock tunnel, the Mont Cenis railroad tunnel, opened in 1871. It extends under the Alps for 13.6 kilometers (8½ miles) to link France and Italy.

Soft-earth tunnels are dug through soil, mud, or soft rock. To prevent the roof and sides of the tunnel from caving in during

A huge drill-like machine digs an underwater tunnel. Air under high pressure keeps the tunnel from leaking. Men must enter and leave the tunnel through special air locks.

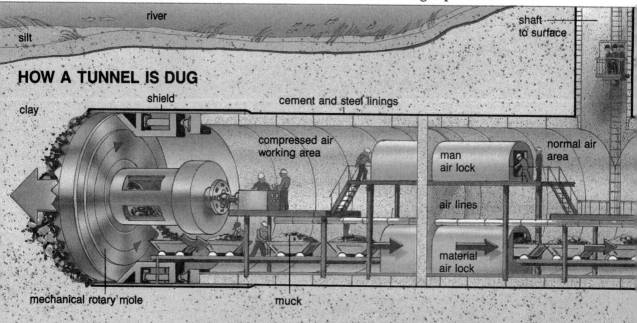

HOW A TUNNEL IS DUG

river

shaft to surface

silt

clay

shield

cement and steel linings

compressed air working area

man air lock

normal air area

air lines

material air lock

mechanical rotary mole

muck

construction, a *shield* is used. The shield is like a gigantic metal pipe, open at both ends. The sharp front edge cuts into the soft earth, and workers remove the dirt. Each time the shield moves ahead, the workers build a section of tunnel wall behind it.

Underwater tunnels are the most difficult to construct because of the risk of flooding. Workers dig a wide shaft straight down into the ground beneath a river or bay. An airtight shield is lowered through the shaft and closed. Compressed air is pumped into it until the pressure of the air pushing out from the inside equals the pressure of the water. This prevents water from seeping in.

To enter the pressurized shield, workers pass through chambers called *locks.* The air pressure in the locks increases gradually, so the workers' bodies have a chance to adjust. Once inside the shield, the workers begin digging the tunnel horizontally. They construct steel-and-concrete supports strong enough to resist the water pressure. The air pressure in completed sections of the tunnel is returned to normal. When leaving the pressurized work area, the workers must again pass through the locks.

Cut-and-cover tunnels are usually shallow tunnels, such as those used for subways. To build them, workers dig a wide, deep trench. The tunnel is constructed in the trench and covered with soil. If the tunnel is to be underwater, a trench is dredged across the

bottom. Sections of the tunnel, already put together, are floated over the trench on barges. Work crews lower the sections and divers fasten them together. When all the sections are connected, water is pumped out of the finished tube. Workers wait until the insides are dry, then finish off the tunnel.

Turkey

Capital: Ankara
Area: 301,381 square miles (780,577 square kilometers)
Population (1985): about 50,661,000
Official language: Turkish

Turkey is a large country in the Middle East. It faces the Mediterranean Sea to the south, and the Black Sea to the north. The northwestern tip of Turkey is in Europe. At the western end of the country, three narrow water passages—the Bosporus, the Dardanelles, and the Sea of Marmara—connect the

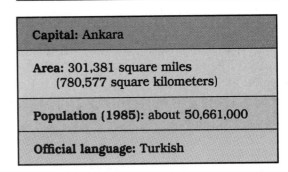

Black and Mediterranean seas. Ships use these waterways to reach ports along the Black Sea.

Turkey has about twice as much land as California and nearly twice as many people. It stretches about 1,000 miles (1,600 kilometers) from east to west. Turkey is an important crossroads for Europe, the Middle East, and Asia.

Most of Turkey's land is mountainous and dry. But along seacoasts and in mountain valleys, farmers grow wheat, cotton, tobacco, and other crops. Grapes for wine are grown in the European portion of Turkey. Cattle, goats, and sheep graze where the land is too rugged for farming. Industry is becoming more and more important to Turkey. But more than half of all Turks still live in the countryside.

Turkey has two great cities. Ankara, near the middle of the country, is the capital. Istanbul, in the far west, is one of the world's most historic cities. In ancient times, it was known as Byzantium. In the year 330, the Roman emperor Constantine the Great renamed it Constantinople and made it the capital of the eastern Roman Empire. It remained the capital for nearly 1,000 years.

In 1453, Constantinople was conquered by a group of Turks known as the Ottomans.

Istanbul is on the Bosporus, the passage between the Mediterranean and Black seas.

They renamed the city Istanbul and made it their capital. They built many *mosques* —Muslim places of worship—in the city. The Ottomans conquered a huge empire and continued to rule Turkey for 400 years. Islam is still the religion of most Turks.

A leader named Kemal ended the Ottoman Empire in 1922 and began the modern country of Turkey. He helped set up a new written language and encouraged people to go to school and learn modern skills. Because of his leadership, Kemal earned a new last name—Ataturk, which means "father of the Turks."

In 1945, the Soviet Union wanted to sign a treaty of friendship with Turkey by which Turkey would give up some territory and allow Soviet military bases on Turkish soil. Turkey refused and asked the United States and European countries for help. Since then, Turkey has been a U.S. ally.

turkey

The turkey is a large bird. Wild turkeys are found only in North and Central America. Hundreds of years ago, American Indians began to raise turkeys for food. Today, turkey farming is an important industry, and turkey meat is a popular food in many parts of the world. Many Americans celebrate Thanksgiving with a turkey dinner.

A turkey does not have feathers on its head and neck. It has a fold of skin called a *wattle* hanging from its throat.

Wild turkeys live in wooded areas and often roost in trees at night. During the day, they search the ground for food—mostly seeds, nuts, and insects. They have strong legs and are good runners. But they are not strong fliers. An adult wild turkey weighs about 8 kilograms (17½ pounds). They are smaller than *domestic* turkeys—those raised on farms.

Some domestic turkeys weigh up to 27 kilograms (60 pounds). They have been bred to have a meatier breast and shorter legs than wild turkeys have.

A turkey has a pouch of skin called a *snood* that hangs over its bill.

Male turkeys—also called *toms*—are bigger than females and have large tail feathers. When the males court the females—called *hens*—they spread their tail feathers into a wide fan. Then they puff and call "Gobble, gobble, gobble." The gobbling can be heard far away.

turtle

The turtle is an animal related to snakes, lizards, and other reptiles. The turtle is a *cold-blooded* animal. Its body temperature depends on the temperature of its surroundings. Turtles must *hibernate* when temperatures get too cold. When the weather gets very hot, some turtles *estivate*—go into a sort of sleep that resembles hibernation. (*See* **hibernation.**)

A turtle has a hard shell that protects the soft inner parts of its body. This is very important for the slow-moving turtle, because it cannot escape danger by running quickly.

A turtle shell has two parts. One part covers the back, and the other covers the belly. The two parts are connected along the sides. Inside, the turtle's backbone and ribs are connected to the shell. There is an opening at the front end for the turtle's head, an opening at the back end for the tail, and openings along the sides for the legs. Some kinds of turtles can pull their entire bodies into the shells, and then completely close the openings. Other kinds cannot pull in their legs.

Turtles are protected by their shells. The snapping turtle also has strong jaws. The stinkpot has a disagreeable smell, and the leatherback is a strong swimmer.

alligator snapping turtle

stinkpot
(musk turtle)

leatherback turtle

Turtles do not have teeth. Instead, the edges of their jaws are sharp and horny. Turtles use this *beak* to cut food into small pieces. Most turtles eat both plant and animal matter, but some eat only plants and others eat only animals.

There are about 250 kinds of turtles. The largest is the leatherback. This sea turtle may be 2.5 meters (8 feet) long and weigh more than 680 kilograms (1,500 pounds). Other turtles, such as the musk turtle, are quite small, weighing less than 0.75 kilograms (1 pound).

Some turtles live on land, and others live in fresh water or the sea. Land turtles are often called *tortoises*. They have high, rounded shells. Land turtles may live for many years. Some land turtles in zoos have lived for more than 100 years. Turtles that live in water have more streamlined shapes, and webbed feet or legs shaped like paddles or flippers. This helps them swim.

All turtles lay their eggs on land. The female digs a nest for the eggs in the ground or in damp sand. After laying the eggs, she covers them and leaves. When the babies hatch, they must care for themselves. Baby land and pond turtles do not have many enemies. But baby sea turtles are attacked by gulls and other birds. Few of them make it from the nest to the sea.

People hunt turtles for their meat and shells. Some turtles were hunted so much that now they are extinct. Other kinds—especially certain sea turtles—are rare and in great danger of becoming extinct. It is hard for them to find a quiet beach where they can lay their eggs. Some kinds are now protected by laws.

Tutankhamen

Tutankhamen (toot-ahnk-AH-mun) was a *pharaoh*—a king of ancient Egypt. He was born around 1370 B.C. and became pharaoh when he was about 9 years old. He died at age 18 and is famous today for his magnificent tomb.

A gold mask of Tutankhamen was part of the coffin that contained his mummified body.

In 1922, Howard Carter, an English archaeologist, cleared away the rubble that blocked the entrance to the tomb. He found things almost as they had been when the tomb was sealed, more than 3,000 years ago.

The outer room held golden couches, beds, and lamps, and the pharaoh's chariot and throne. The gold and silver throne was covered in brilliant jewels. A second room contained golden statues. A sealed third room revealed Tutankhamen's coffins. There were three coffins, one inside the other. The innermost coffin was solid gold and shaped like Tutankhamen. The *mummy*—his wrapped and carefully preserved body—rested inside. A gold mask covered the mummy's face. The mask is decorated with rows of blue stones. A few years later, a fourth room was opened. This room contained even more treasures. (*See* **mummy**.)

Many of the tomb's beautiful objects may be seen in the Cairo Museum in Egypt.

Tuvalu, *see* Pacific Islands

Twain, Mark

Mark Twain was one of America's greatest and funniest writers. His many books include *The Adventures of Tom Sawyer, The Adventures of Huckleberry Finn, A Connecticut Yankee in King Arthur's Court,* and *The Prince and the Pauper.*

Twain was born in 1835 in Missouri. His real name was Samuel Clemens. As a young man, he worked as a Mississippi riverboat pilot. The boatmen used to call out "Mark twain!"—meaning that the water was about six feet deep. When he began to write, Clemens signed his works "Mark Twain."

In 1865, Twain published his first successful story—"The Celebrated Jumping Frog of Calaveras County." It is about a frog-jumping contest in California. The story made Twain famous in the East.

Twain toured the world, gave lectures, and wrote many more books and articles. He became widely known as one of America's funniest men and best writers. But the last 20 years of Twain's life were not very happy. His wife and two of his daughters died, he lost a lot of money, and his health became poor. Twain died in 1910.

Today, Twain's books are enjoyed by children and adults. *Huckleberry Finn* is considered his greatest book. The story is told by 12-year-old Huck. He and Jim, a runaway black slave, travel on a raft down the Mississippi River. Huck tries to help Jim escape to freedom, but Jim is captured. They later find out that Jim's owner has died and freed him in her will.

A Connecticut Yankee in King Arthur's Court is the story of a a New England man of the 1800s. He wakes up one day to find himself in England during the days of King Arthur. He has many hair-raising adventures, and uses his scientific knowledge to save himself. He creates so much confusion that Merlin the magician gladly sends him back to his own time.

The Prince and the Pauper takes place in England in the 1500s. It is the story of

Huckleberry Finn

Connecticut Yankee

Celebrated Jumping Frog

riverboat

young Prince Edward and poor Tom—the pauper. The two boys look exactly alike, so they switch clothes and places. Tom enjoys the royal life, and Edward discovers what life is like for the common people.

See also **Tom Sawyer.**

Tyler, John, *see* presidents of the U.S.

typewriter

The typewriter is a machine that prints letters and symbols. There are three main kinds of typewriters—*manual, electric,* and *electronic.*

A manual typewriter is powered by the *typist*—the person operating it. Each key is connected by a thin rod to a piece of metal type. Pressing a key makes the type strike an inked ribbon and leave a mark on the paper.

A *carriage* moves the paper from left to right so the letters print one after the other. Electric typewriters work like manuals, except that an electric motor moves the rods when the typist presses the keys. This makes typing easier and faster.

An electronic typewriter has a *printing element*—a ball covered with raised characters. As keys are pressed, electronic signals turn the printing element so the desired characters strike the ribbon. The carriage does not move. Instead, the printing element moves. Electronic typewriters have computers that store what has been typed. Many have a display to let the typist check the typing and make corrections before printing.

Computers called *word processors* now do much of the work once done by typewriters. A word processor has a keyboard very much like a typewriter keyboard. People who type material on a word processor are called *keyboarders.* (*See* **computer.**)

An early manual typewriter and a modern electronic typewriter (below) have the same keyboard arrangement (right). The top row of letters is "QWERTYUIOP."

The letter *U* began as an Egyptian word picture. The Semites called it *waw*, meaning "hook."

The Romans used this symbol, like our letter *V*, for both the *U* and the *V* sounds.

In the Middle Ages, people who copied books made the letter *U* curved at the bottom.

Uganda, *see* Africa

ultraviolet light

Ultraviolet light is a form of electromagnetic radiation. Ordinary light and radio waves are other forms of electromagnetic radiation. Humans cannot see ultraviolet light, so it is sometimes called *black light*. Bees and some other insects can see it.

The waves of ultraviolet light are longer than those of X rays but shorter than those of violet light, the shortest visible light waves. *Ultra-* means "beyond." Ultraviolet light is just beyond violet light in the electromagnetic spectrum.

Most ultraviolet light comes from the sun. Much of it is absorbed by the protective ozone layer of Earth's atmosphere, and a small amount reaches the ground. Most living things need some exposure to ultraviolet light. People need it to produce vitamin D. But too much exposure causes sunburn, weakens the immune system, and can cause skin cancer.

Ultraviolet light can be produced by lamps and arc lights. These have many uses in laboratories and industry. Ultraviolet lamps are sometimes used to kill germs.

See also **color** and **light**.

Underground Railroad

The Underground Railroad helped 60,000 to 70,000 American slaves escape to freedom. It was a secret network of roads, paths, and waterways that led from the southern United States, through the North, and to Canada. It also included the many people who guided the runaway slaves. It was used from the early 1800s to 1860.

Before slavery was outlawed in 1865, about 4 million black slaves lived in the southern United States. Many people in the North and South were against slavery. They set up a way to help the slaves flee. It was dangerous for both the slaves and their helpers. The slaves were not safe until they reached Canada. By law, even slaves caught in the North had to be returned to their owners. People who helped runaway slaves could be arrested.

Runaway slaves traveled at night and hid during the day at "stations"—safe places

People in a snowy northern town give shelter to slaves traveling to Canada.

where they received food and rest. People known as "conductors" helped the runaways travel from station to station. The conductors were often former slaves. Harriet Tubman, for example, worked for the Underground Railroad after she escaped from slavery. (*See* **Tubman, Harriet.**)

See also **slavery.**

underwater sports

Underwater sports allow people to see the world of undersea plants and animals. Two kinds of underwater sports are *scuba diving* (also called *skin diving)* and *snorkeling.*

A scuba diver carries air-filled tanks and swims below the water's surface. The scuba diver also wears a wet suit, a weighted belt, flippers, a face mask, a watch, a pressure gauge, and a knife. The tight-fitting wet suit covers the whole body and keeps the diver warm. The flippers make swimming easier. The watch and pressure gauge help divers judge how deep they may go and how long

they may stay down. The deeper they go and the longer they stay down, the more air is used. Below a certain depth, the pressure is so great that a diver can safely remain there only a short time.

A scuba diver takes lessons to learn to breathe properly and to use the equipment. A diver has to learn how to *descend*—go down—and *ascend*—come up—slowly, so that the pressure inside the body can adjust to the pressure outside.

A snorkeler breathes through a short pipe called a *snorkel.* Since the snorkel must extend above the water, a snorkeler swims near the surface. A snorkeler also wears a face mask and flippers. Snorkeling is easy to learn and fairly safe.

See also **diving.**

uniform

A uniform is special clothing worn by certain workers and by members of special groups and organizations. Soldiers, police

A scuba diver (bottom) carries a supply of air and can dive deep into the water. A snorkeler (top) breathes through a short snorkel and stays near the surface.

British soldiers were called "redcoats" because of the color of their uniform (left). Summer campers wear an informal uniform (right)—the camp tee shirt.

officers, fire fighters, letter carriers, and medical workers wear uniforms. Students who attend private schools often wear uniforms. Waiters and waitresses usually wear uniforms. Many athletes wear uniforms.

Some uniforms consist of an entire outfit, including hat and shoes. Others are just a few items, such as a hat, badge, or special jacket. Besides being in a certain style or color, many uniforms are designed for comfort and protection.

The word *uniform* means "all the same." When people wear uniforms, they show that they are members of a certain group. For some people, wearing a uniform gives them a way to show they are proud of their group.

People in charge of an organization or who do special jobs may have uniforms that are slightly different. Army generals and police captains, for example, wear uniforms that regular soldiers and police officers may not wear. This is so that they may be identified easily. Special uniforms also honor those who have reached a high level—*rank*—in the group.

Military Uniforms When people think of uniforms, they often picture military clothes. Military uniforms started to appear in the 1500s. Before that time, a soldier often wore a special color or design on his clothes that identified him with his leader. He did not wear a complete uniform.

During the 1500s, many kings had their guards wear splendid uniforms. Other groups then began to wear uniforms, too. These outfits were often colorful and expensive. They were usually very heavy and uncomfortable.

British soldiers began to wear red coats in the 1600s. Each *regiment*—division—of the army wore its own colors inside the red coat. Other European armies also dressed their soldiers in bright, fancy uniforms at this time. Often, only officers and regular soldiers wore full uniforms. People who were *drafted* —forced to fight—usually wore their own clothes or parts of a uniform.

Armies used to charge each other and fight on the open battlefield. By World War I, the ways of fighting wars had changed. Soldiers stayed hidden. A bright uniform was dangerous, because it was easy to spot against the ground or trees. To provide better camouflage, most modern-day fighting uniforms come in shades of green, tan, and *khaki*—a yellow-brown color. Soldiers usually have several uniforms. One uniform is worn when fighting or training. A *dress uniform* is worn for special occasions. Women's military uniforms are usually the same colors as those worn by men. Sailors' uniforms are often dark blue or white.

Team Uniforms Most sports teams wear uniforms. At first, athletes wore uniforms during games just to show which team they were on. Later, parts of uniforms were designed to protect players against injuries. Helmets are now part of the uniforms for baseball, football, and thoroughbred horse racing. Football and hockey uniforms include protective pads.

Cheerleaders and members of marching bands and drill teams dress in uniforms, too. The colors of their uniforms show which school, team, or organization they represent.

Work Uniforms Most police officers and fire fighters wear uniforms and badges. This helps people quickly identify them. Fire fighters' uniforms also are worn for protection. They are made of materials that do not burn easily. Their hats, coats, and boots are waterproof. The hard hat also protects the head from falling objects.

Many other people wear uniforms as part of their jobs. For example, nurses who serve patients in hospitals often work in *sterile* —germ-free—surroundings. A clean nurse's uniform suggests that the wearer is also clean.

Airplane pilots, flight attendants, railroad conductors, and some bus drivers also wear uniforms. So do school-crossing guards, car-rental agents, and people in many other jobs. The uniform helps people tell who is supposed to perform a job.

Uniforms for Young People Young people who belong to certain groups or clubs wear uniforms. Boy Scouts and Girl Scouts have uniforms. Some Scouts wear a whole outfit. Others may wear just a cap or sash. Many other youth groups have uniforms or special jackets, caps, or ties.

Some schools require their students to wear uniforms. In the United States, most public-school students do not wear uniforms. In many other countries, all students are expected to wear school uniforms. Camps and other groups may also have young people wear uniforms. This helps build team spirit.

United Arab Emirates, *see* Middle East

United Kingdom

Capital: London
Area: 94,226 square miles (244,045 square kilometers)
Population (1985): about 56,422,000
Official language: English

The United Kingdom is an island nation in northwestern Europe. It is often called Great Britain because most of the country occupies the large island of Great Britain. Its official name is the United Kingdom of Great Britain and Northern Ireland.

Altogether, the United Kingdom has about two-thirds as much land as California and about twice as many people. But its importance is far greater than its size. For 200 years, the United Kingdom was among the most powerful countries on Earth. It owned colonies in North America and Australia, and once controlled nearly half of Africa and all of the huge subcontinent of India. It spread the English language to all of these regions, making English the most widely spoken language in the world.

Today, the United Kingdom is less powerful. People still come to Britain from many other countries. Some come to live and find jobs. Many come to study at the great British universities.

The United Kingdom has four main divisions—England, Scotland, Wales, and

London's famous Big Ben clock tower (right) is part of the Houses of Parliament.

Northern Ireland. In some ways, these parts are like states in the United States. In other ways, they are like separate countries. Each has its own traditions and history.

England England takes up the southern part of the island of Great Britain. It is the largest part of the United Kingdom. More than 47 million of the United Kingdom's people—about 82 out of 100—live in England. Most live in or near large cities.

England gets its name from the Angles, a tribe that settled in Britain in the 600s,

At left, Queen Elizabeth II (on balcony in pink dress) reviews a British honor guard. At right, a street in Cardiff, the largest city in Wales.

along with the Saxons and the Jutes. Beginning in the late 1500s, England became a powerful kingdom. Its sailors began trade with many parts of the world. England also set up colonies, including the colonies that later became the United States and Canada.

England also worked to control its own island of Great Britain. In 1707, England, Wales, and Scotland were joined under a single government and called the United Kingdom. Later, Northern Ireland became part of the United Kingdom.

Steam-powered factories were first developed in England. These factories produced cloth and other goods faster and more cheaply. Central England was soon dotted with large industrial cities. England sold its manufactured goods around the world. (*See* **Industrial Revolution.**)

England's largest city is London, one of the most important cities in the world. It is the capital of the United Kingdom and is a major center of world trade and culture, especially drama. (*See* **London.**)

Wales Wales is a mountainous region in western Great Britain. It is surrounded on three sides by water. It has about 3 million people—about 5 out of every 100 in the United Kingdom. Cardiff is the capital.

The Welsh have held on to many of their customs and traditions. Most speak English, but many also speak Welsh, a Celtic language related to languages spoken in Ireland and Scotland. (*See* **Celts.**)

Ancestors of the Welsh lived in Great Britain more than 2,000 years ago. They were conquered by the Romans around the time of Christ. Later, Angles, Saxons, Celts, Normans, and English peoples arrived. The Welsh fought bravely against these invaders, but in 1536, Wales came under English rule.

Wales is famous for its productive coal mines and for its green countryside. Ocean currents keep the weather moist and mild throughout the year. The Welsh are known as great singers, and there are large festivals where singing groups compete. One famous Welsh tune is known in America as the lullaby "All Through the Night."

Scotland Scotland occupies the northern part of the island of Great Britain and hundreds of nearby islands. Scotland has over 5 million people. About 9 people out of every 100 in the United Kingdom live in

At left, the green countryside of Northern Ireland is typical of much of the United Kingdom. At right, a small harbor in Scotland.

Scotland. Most live near Scotland's narrow "waist," formed by deep *firths.* Scotland's two large cities, Glasgow and Edinburgh, lie at the edge of firths. Edinburgh is Scotland's capital.

To the north are the wild and beautiful Highlands, where cattle and sheep graze. *Lochs*—long, deep lakes—lie between the mountains.

Some Highlanders speak Scots Gaelic, a Celtic language related to those spoken in Wales and Ireland. The men sometimes wear skirtlike *kilts.* The bagpipe is a popular instrument for Scottish music.

In the 500s, several peoples in northern Britain joined to form the first Scottish kingdom. For centuries, the Scots were independent. Beginning around the year 1100, England began trying to make Scotland a part of its own territory. England and Scotland opposed each other for 600 years— sometimes peacefully and sometimes in war. England was the bigger and richer of the two, and in 1707, Scotland agreed to a union. It dissolved its own government and sent elected representatives to the national government in London.

Many heroes of Scottish legend were warriors who defeated the English. Robert the Bruce led a revolt against England and defeated English armies at Bannockburn in 1314. He became King Robert I of Scotland.

Northern Ireland Northern Ireland takes up the northeast corner of the island of Ireland. It is sometimes called Ulster, though it does not include all the land once known as Ulster. The rest of the island is occupied by the independent Republic of Ireland. (*See* **Ireland.**)

About 1½ million people live in Northern Ireland—about 3 people out of every 100 in the United Kingdom. It is a beautiful land of rolling hills, plains, and low mountains. Its deep inlets provide excellent harbors. Belfast, Northern Ireland's former capital and chief city, has one of the world's best natural harbors.

From 1541 to 1922, Britain claimed to rule all of Ireland. The British tried to introduce Protestant Christianity as it was practiced in England. But the Irish, who were Roman Catholics, revolted against the British over and over again. In 1922, most of Ireland became an independent nation.

But many people in the six northeastern counties wanted to remain part of the United Kingdom. Most were Protestants, whose ancestors had come to Ireland from England or Scotland. Though the Roman Catholics who lived there wanted to join the Irish Republic, the northeastern counties became Northern Ireland.

For decades, Protestants and Roman Catholics in Northern Ireland have clashed with each other. The government, controlled by Protestants, dealt harshly with Roman Catholics. Hard times in the shipbuilding and textile industries made tensions worse. Social and economic differences have followed upon religious differences. The two sides still disagree over the political future of Ulster. Each side continues to lash out violently against the other.

The United Kingdom Today The people of the United Kingdom have many differences. But they also have much to hold them together.

The main symbol of the United Kingdom is the *monarchy*—the British queen or king. The monarch is the *head of state*—the person who represents the kingdom. Even people who oppose the elected government pledge allegiance to the monarch.

Government decisions are made by *Parliament,* which is somewhat like the U.S. Congress. People in all parts of the United Kingdom elect Members of Parliament. These representatives meet in London to pass laws and take care of other business.

The United Kingdom has no president. The most powerful government officer is the prime minister, elected by Parliament.

See also **English language** and **English history.**

United Nations

The United Nations (U.N.) is an organization made up of almost all the countries of the world. The member nations work together to preserve peace and improve living conditions around the world.

The United Nations Secretariat building in New York City.

World War II was still going on when China, Great Britain, the Soviet Union, and the United States began planning a worldwide peacekeeping organization. Many people living then had experienced two terrible wars—World War I (1914 to 1917) and World War II (started in 1939). They wanted

Nearly every nation sends a representative to the U.N. General Assembly each fall.

to prevent wars like these from happening again.

In 1945, representatives from 50 nations met in San Francisco, California, to write the United Nations charter. This document described the purposes and operation of the organization. The charter was signed by 51 nations. Today, over 150 nations belong to the United Nations.

Organization The U.N. is made up of a number of special groups and agencies. Among these are the General Assembly, the Security Council, and the Economic and Social Council (ECOSOC). These three bodies can create other, smaller agencies to deal with particular problems. The Secretariat is a fourth major branch of the United Nations. It is made up of people who perform the day-to-day work of the United Nations. Administrators, project directors, and translators are some of the people who work for the Secretariat.

The General Assembly is made up of representatives of all the member nations. At General Assembly meetings, members discuss issues of concern to the U.N. and its members. They elect members to the other, smaller U.N. groups and decide how to spend the U.N.'s budget. Decisions are made by voting. Each nation has one vote.

The Security Council has 15 member nations. Five are permanent members—Great Britain, China, France, the Soviet Union, and the United States. The other ten are elected by the General Assembly for two-year terms. The Security Council can suggest ways to settle disputes. It can also order action against a nation that threatens world peace. All five permanent members must approve any Security Council decision.

The Economic and Social Council works to improve how people live. Its many programs help less-developed nations share in the scientific, medical, technical, and agricultural knowledge of more-developed nations. It has 54 members, each elected by the General Assembly to serve for three years.

The U.N.'s many special agencies send workers all over the world. Perhaps the best known of these agencies is the United Nations Children's Fund (UNICEF). Two others are the ECOSOC's World Health Organization (WHO) and its United Nations Educational, Scientific, and Cultural Organization (UNESCO).

Improving Living Conditions About four-fifths of the U.N.'s money is used to improve health and living conditions around the world. One form of help is technical assistance. U.N. teams have taught villagers

At left, U.N. advisers helped a village pump water from a well for irrigation.
At right, the soldiers from U.N. member countries in Lebanon to help keep peace.

in poor nations how to dig wells and build schools. In other countries, U.N. advisers have helped people build factories.

A major goal of the U.N. is to end hunger. U.N. agencies have helped poor nations grow more food. The U.N. has also distributed food to areas where people are starving.

The World Health Organization has drained swamps to prevent the spread of malaria. It has vaccinated thousands of people against polio and smallpox. It collects information on diseases and epidemics.

The U.N. cares for *refugees*—people forced from their homelands by war. Since 1948, the U.N. has supplied food, shelter, and medical care for Palestinians made homeless in the Middle East. In 1981, the Office of the United Nations High Commissioner for Refugees was awarded a Nobel Peace Prize for helping millions of Vietnamese refugees.

Peacekeeping The United Nations has helped nations settle their disputes. Nations can talk about their differences during General Assembly meetings. When member nations have gone to war, the U.N. General Assembly has sometimes asked for a *cease-fire*—a halt to the fighting. This gives the nations a chance to reach an agreement. Member nations will also send armed forces to guard the borders between nations at war. But the U.N. may send in an army only if the warring nations agree to its presence.

Since the formation of Israel, in 1948, the U.N. has been trying to keep peace between Israel and the Arab nations of the Middle East. In 1950, Ralph J. Bunche, a member of the U.N. Palestine Commission, was awarded the Nobel Peace Prize for his work in arranging cease-fires with Israel and its neighbors.

Visiting the U.N. Member nations have contributed many works of art to make the U.N.'s New York headquarters beautiful. The buildings and garden are open to visitors. Tour guides lead groups of visitors through the U.N. If the General Assembly is in session, you may sit in on a meeting. You can listen through headsets to English translations of the speeches.

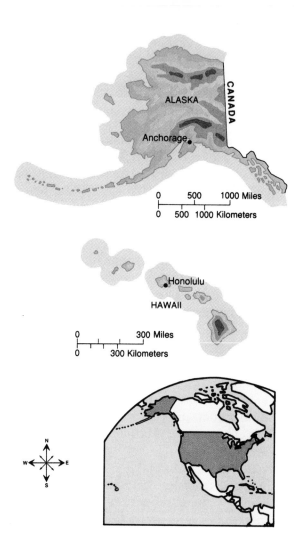

United States

Capital: Washington, D.C.
Area: 3,615,105 square miles (9,363,122 square kilometers)
Population (1980): 227,061,000 (1985): about 238,631,000
Official language: English

The United States of America stretches across the mountains, river valleys, and plains of the North American continent from the Atlantic Ocean in the East to the Pacific Ocean in the West. The United States also includes the tropical island state of Hawaii, and the huge state of Alaska at North America's cold northwestern tip.

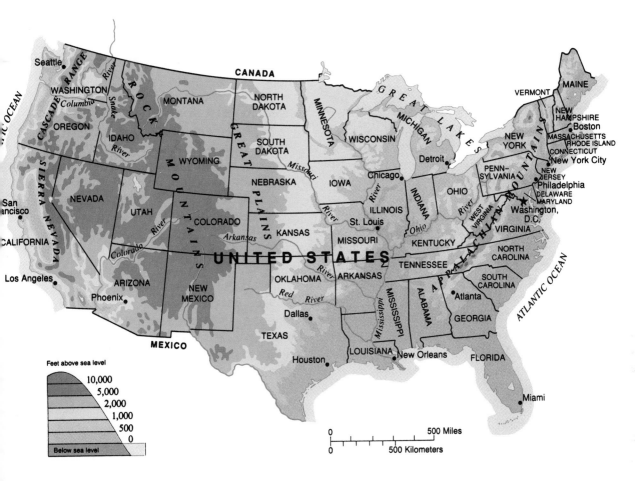

The United States is a vast and varied land. It has some of the world's largest and most exciting cities, and some of its most beautiful and majestic wilderness regions. It is the world's fourth-largest country both in land and in population. Yet the United States is united by a strong central government and has a rich shared culture as well as customs brought from many other lands.

The United States is made up of 50 states and the District of Columbia. The state of Alaska is separated by Canada from the main part of the United States. Hawaii, the newest state, is a group of islands in the Pacific Ocean, about halfway between North America and Asia. The southern part of the continental United States is bordered by Mexico and the Gulf of Mexico. Canada is the country's northern neighbor.

The United States also has some territories and possessions. The largest is Puerto Rico, an island in the Atlantic Ocean about 1,000 miles (1,600 kilometers) southeast of Florida. Puerto Rico is a commonwealth—it is self-governing, but under U.S. law. The U.S. Virgin Islands are in the Atlantic, too. Pacific island possessions include Guam and American Samoa. (*See* **Puerto Rico**; **West Indies**; and **Pacific Islands**.)

If Alaska were placed over the other states, it would stretch from Canada to Mexico!

The capital of the United States is the city of Washington, in the District of Columbia. This is a small area of land about halfway down the Atlantic coast between Maryland and Virginia. (*See* **Washington, D.C.**)

Land   Much of the eastern and southeastern United States is a coastal lowland, with rich farmlands. The Appalachian Highlands, a chain of low mountains and rolling uplands, runs southwestward from Maine to Alabama. (*See* **Appalachian Mountains.**)

A large area of land called the *plains* lies between the Appalachian Highlands in the East and the Rocky Mountains in the West. The northern plains are covered with lakes and forests. The eastern plains are good for farming. Corn and soybeans are the major crops. The Great Plains lie farther west. Here, the land is dry and flat. Wheat is grown in the fertile areas. Beef cattle and other livestock graze on the vast grasslands of the Great Plains. (*See* **Great Plains.**)

The Rocky Mountains are made up of mountain ranges and broad, flat valleys. An imaginary line called the *continental* *divide* runs through the Rocky Mountains. East of the continental divide, streams flow into the Gulf of Mexico, an arm of the Atlantic Ocean. West of the divide, they flow into the Pacific Ocean. (*See* **Rocky Mountains** and **continental divide.**)

West of the Rockies are plateaus and wide open stretches of land. Little rain falls, and only desert plants grow in most of this area. The region includes California's Death Valley, the driest and lowest spot in the United States. Less than 2 inches (5 centimeters) of rain falls in Death Valley each year, and it lies 282 feet (86 meters) below sea level. (*See* **Death Valley.**)

The Pacific Mountain System runs through Alaska, Washington, Oregon, and California. It includes the Cascade Mountains in the North and the Sierra Nevada in the South. Thick forests cover parts of the Cascades. Mount St. Helens, an active volcano, is part of this range. The highest point in North America is Alaska's Mount McKinley. It rises 20,320 feet (6,194 meters) above sea level. (*See* **Pacific Mountain System.**)

Americans include children and grandparents, workers who build and produce things, and artists who make music or create beautiful objects.

The United States has some of the world's largest rivers and lakes. They are used to transport goods and create electric power. Parts of these waterways are set aside as recreational areas. The Mississippi River flows southward from northern Minnesota to the Gulf of Mexico. It is the longest river in the United States. The Mississippi and its *tributaries*—the rivers that flow into it—drain most of the land between the Appalachian and Rocky mountains. This is about one-third of the United States. Food crops, industrial products, and raw materials are shipped along the Mississippi River System. (*See* **Mississippi River.**)

To the north lie the five Great Lakes. Together, the Great Lakes make up the largest body of fresh water in the world. Four of these lakes form the border between the United States and Canada. The canals and locks built to connect all five lakes make them an excellent waterway even for large ships. The Great Lakes are linked to the Atlantic Ocean by the St. Lawrence Seaway, and to the Mississippi River System by the Illinois Waterway. (*See* **Great Lakes** and **St. Lawrence River.**)

Natural Resources The United States is especially rich in fertile land, forests, and mineral deposits. Its highways, railroads, waterways, and air transportation system allow goods to be shipped quickly and reliably. This has made the United States one of the world's leading producers of agricultural and manufactured goods.

Fewer than three out of every hundred workers in the United States are farmers, but they produce more food than the nation needs. The principal crop is corn. Wheat, barley, oats, potatoes, soybeans, fruits, and vegetables are other important food crops. Cotton and tobacco are important nonfood crops.

Dairy farming is another leading agricultural activity. The United States produces twice as much milk as any other country, and it is the world's leading producer of cheese. Many kinds of livestock are raised for meat. Texas, Iowa, and Nebraska lead in the production of beef cattle.

The most important metal mined in the United States is iron. Iron and the steel made from it are used in many industries. The United States ranks second in the world in the production of petroleum and coal. Other minerals are copper, lead, and uranium.

Forests in the Pacific Northwest, the South, and the Northeast supply lumber for furniture and other wood products, such as paper. Fishing is an important activity along the Atlantic and Pacific coasts and in the Gulf of Mexico.

Manufacturing employs more Americans than does any other economic activity. The major products are metals, machinery, automobiles and other transportation equipment, processed food, and clothing. The Northeast and the Midwest are the two largest manufacturing areas in the country. Together, these two regions have more than half of the nation's factories and workers.

People Indian peoples moved from Asia into North America about 14,000 years ago. The ancestors of today's black Americans came from Africa. Many of them were brought to North America to work as slaves. They began arriving in the early 1600s. Many white Americans are descended from the Spanish, French, British, Germans, and other Europeans who settled North America hundreds of years ago. (*See* **Indians, American** and **black Americans.**)

Even though cities do not cover much of the land, about four-fifths of all Americans live in or around them. A city and its suburbs form what is called a *metropolitan area*. The nation's largest metropolitan area is New York. Seven out of every hundred Americans live in or near New York City. (*See* **New York City.**)

Millions of Americans live in and around the cities of Los Angeles, California; Chicago, Illinois; Houston, Texas; and Philadelphia, Pennsylvania. In recent years, many people have moved from the colder climate of the Northeast to the warmer "Sunbelt" states of the South and Southwest. (*See* **Atlanta; Dallas;** and **Los Angeles.**)

The United States is often called a "nation of immigrants." This is because so many Americans either were born in another country or are descended from people who immigrated to the United States, seeking freedom and a better life. The nation was founded by immigrants from Europe. During the 1700s, 1800s, and early 1900s, most immigrants came from Europe. Today, many come from Asia and South and Central America. (*See* **immigration.**)

When the American people were counted in 1980, the results showed that five out of every hundred people had been born in another country. The greatest numbers came from Mexico, Germany, Canada, Italy, Great Britain, Cuba, the Philippines, Poland, and the Soviet Union.

The people of the United States are therefore a blend of many peoples. They practice traditions, customs, and religions from all over the world. Some groups, though, have kept their own customs, languages, and ways of cooking, and have not borrowed from other groups living here.

Government The government of the United States is divided into the federal government, 50 state governments, and many local governments. Local governments manage counties, metropolitan areas, cities, towns, and villages. Each of these governments is run as a democracy and according to the laws written in its constitution or charter. In all of the governments, officials are elected or appointed. They serve for a certain number of years. Laws are usually made by a group of elected representatives. Sometimes, during a state election, people vote to pass a law. Disputes can be settled in a court of law, and anyone accused of a crime may defend himself or herself in a trial.

See also **United States history.** See the Index for entries on the individual states.

United States history

More than 14,000 years ago, peoples who were hunters and gatherers started moving from Asia into North America. They formed tribes and eventually spread over all of North, Central, and South America.

In 1492, Christopher Columbus and the men who sailed with him reached the Americas. Thinking they had found the Indies, they called the people they met in America "Indians." Soon, other Europeans came to claim areas of the New World for their countries. Spain and Portugal wanted South and Central America. Spain, France, England, and the Netherlands all claimed parts of North America. (*See* **Columbus, Christopher** and **Indians, American.**)

Colonizing North America Explorers were followed by trappers, traders, missionaries, and settlers. In 1565, the Spanish founded St. Augustine in Florida. They also settled in what are today Texas, California, New Mexico, and Arizona. The French established colonies and trading posts in what is now Canada, in the Great Lakes region, and along the Mississippi River. The Dutch founded New Netherland in the Hudson River valley, in what is now New York State.

There were Dutch and Swedish settlements in what became New Jersey.

People from England founded most of the colonies that later formed the United States. The first lasting English settlement was started in 1607 at Jamestown, in the colony of Virginia. The settlers had come looking for gold. (*See* **Jamestown.**)

In 1620, an English religious group landed in Massachusetts. Their goal was not riches, but a place where they could worship in their own way. They founded Plymouth Colony. Later, they became known as the Pilgrims. (*See* **Pilgrims** and **Plymouth.**)

A few years later, the Puritans, another religious group, arrived in Massachusetts seeking religious freedom. They founded several villages, which all belonged to the Massachusetts Bay Colony. Boston was the colony's capital. (*See* **Puritans.**)

People from Massachusetts founded the colonies of Connecticut, Rhode Island, and New Hampshire. These four colonies became known as the New England Colonies. The English seized New Netherland and the New Jersey settlements in 1664. New Netherland was renamed New York. New York, New Jersey, Delaware, and Pennsylvania made up the Middle Colonies. Virginia, Maryland, North Carolina, South Carolina, and Georgia were in the South. Maryland and Pennsylvania were set up as colonies where people could worship in ways outlawed in England. By 1770, over 2 million people lived in the 13 colonies. (*See* **colonial life in America; Penn, William;** and **Williams, Roger.**)

Becoming a Nation The colonies were supposed to follow British laws. But the British government left the colonists on their own. The colonists governed themselves. They held town meetings and made their own laws.

France and Britain were enemies in Europe. In North America, they fought the French and Indian War over control of the northern and eastern parts of North America. Most Indians sided with the French and suffered when Britain won it. After the war ended in 1763, the British government decided to take greater control of the colonies. Parliament, the British lawmaking body, began to pass laws requiring the colonists to pay taxes. The colonists protested. Since they had no representatives in Parliament, they believed that Parliament had no right to demand taxes from them. Bad feelings

between the British government and the colonists grew.

On March 5, 1770, colonists in Boston teased some British soldiers and threw snowballs at them. Shooting started, and five Americans died. News of this event—the "Boston Massacre"—spread quickly and enraged the colonists. In 1774, 56 representatives from 12 of the colonies met in Philadelphia for the First Continental Congress. The Congress sent a protest to the British government demanding an immediate change in British policies.

By then, many colonists wanted to break all ties with Britain. They began training as soldiers. They called themselves "Minutemen," because they promised to be ready to fight "at a minute's notice." On April 19, 1775, fighting between the British and the Minutemen started in the Massachusetts towns of Lexington and Concord.

In May of that year, the Second Continental Congress met in Philadelphia. It created the Continental Army and appointed George Washington as its commander in chief. The Revolutionary War had begun. (*See* **Bunker Hill; Washington, George;** and **Revolutionary War.**)

One year later, on July 4, 1776, the Continental Congress adopted the Declaration of Independence. The colonies considered themselves separate from Britain. (*See* **Declaration of Independence.**)

In 1781, after five years of fighting, the British surrendered at Yorktown, Virginia. The colonies were now independent states. (*See* **Yorktown.**)

The states united to form a nation. One of the first tasks they faced was writing a constitution describing how the nation should be governed. Writing this constitution was not an easy task. Some people wanted the federal government to be strong. Others favored strong state governments. But in Congress, the small states needed a way to protect themselves from always having to follow the lead of the large states.

In 1789, the nation adopted the United States Constitution and elected George Washington its first president. A few years later, ten amendments were added to the Constitution. These amendments are called the Bill of Rights. They state the personal freedoms that the government must protect. (*See* **Constitution of the United States** and **Bill of Rights.**)

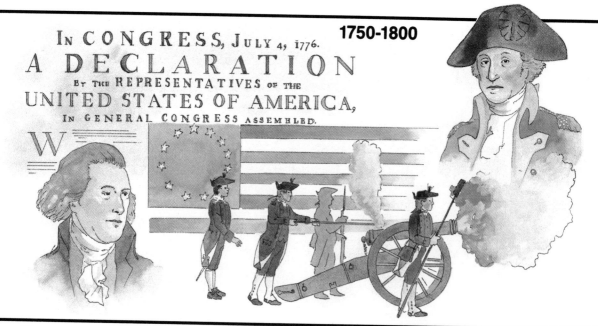

In CONGRESS, July 4, 1776.
A DECLARATION
BY THE REPRESENTATIVES OF THE
UNITED STATES OF AMERICA,
IN GENERAL CONGRESS ASSEMBLED.

1750-1800

Growing Larger and Stronger In 1803, President Thomas Jefferson bought land west of the Mississippi from France. This land is known as the Louisiana Purchase. It doubled the size of the United States. (*See* **Louisiana Purchase.**)

In 1812, the United States again went to war against Britain. The United States had been trading with Britain's enemy, France. The British began seizing U.S. ships at sea. The war ended in 1814, after Britain and France made peace. (*See* **War of 1812.**)

People continued to arrive from Europe. Some settled in the cities along the Atlantic coast. Others crossed the Appalachian Mountains and the Mississippi River, and settled on the plains. The U.S. government forced the Indians to move farther west to *reservations*—lands set aside for them to live on. Within a few years, settlers wanted the reservation lands, too. The Indians fought back. But by the late 1800s, they had been defeated. (*See* **Indian Wars.**)

Americans also moved into areas that belonged to Mexico and set up large ranches. In 1836, the American settlers in Texas founded the independent Republic of Texas. In 1845, Texas joined the United States.

The United States wanted to buy the land west of Texas, but Mexico would not sell. Border disputes came up, and in 1845, the two nations went to war. Two years later, Mexico surrendered. It gave up all of its lands west of Texas. These lands later became the states of California, Arizona, New Mexico, Utah, and Nevada. After the discovery of gold in 1848, thousands of settlers poured into California. It became a state in 1850. The United States now stretched across the continent, all the way from the Atlantic Ocean to the Pacific Ocean. (*See* **Mexican War** and **westward movement.**)

A Nation Divided From colonial times, the North and South had each developed in its own way. The northern economy was based on a variety of activities—farming, crafts, manufacturing, trade, and fishing. The North had waterpower to run its factories. Its cities were busy commercial centers. The southern economy depended mostly on large farms. On these large farms—*plantations*—cotton, tobacco, and indigo were grown. The plantations were worked by slaves. When laws were debated in Congress, the North and South disagreed about many things, especially slavery. Many northerners

1800-1850

THE
EMIGRANTS' GUIDE
TO
CALIFORNIA,

wanted slavery ended, or at least not permitted in the new territories and states. Southerners argued that slaves were needed to keep the economy going. (*See* **slavery**.)

During the 1860 campaign for president, Abraham Lincoln said that slavery should not be allowed in the new settlements of the West. After Lincoln was elected, the southern states left the Union and formed a nation named the Confederate States of America. Lincoln asked the southern states to return to the Union. They refused, and the North and South went to war in 1861. (*See* **Civil War; Confederate States of America;** and **Lincoln, Abraham.**)

The Civil War ended in 1865. General Robert E. Lee, commander of the southern forces, surrendered to General Ulysses S. Grant, commander of the northern forces, at Appomattox Court House in Virginia.

It took the South many years to rebuild its economy after the Civil War. It still had few industries and relied on farming. The freed slaves had an especially hard time finding places to live and work. Federal soldiers stayed in the South during this time, known as the Reconstruction period. The soldiers did not leave until the 1870s. Southerners did not like this at all. It took many years for the hard feelings between the North and South to ease.

Moving onto the World Stage After the Civil War ended, major industries in the North—such as steelmaking and railroad building—grew rapidly. Railroad lines carried raw materials and products across the nation, and telegraph lines carried news cross-country very quickly. Life was transformed in the 1870s by the invention of the telephone, and then electric light. The nation was now able to make all the goods its fast-growing population needed. It sold its extra goods to other nations. By 1900, the United States had become one of the world's richest nations. The owners of the industries became very wealthy.

In 1895, Cuba, a Spanish island 90 miles (150 kilometers) south of the United States, rebelled against Spain. Three years later, the United States joined the Cubans in their fight. The Spanish-American War lasted only for a few months during 1898. When the war was over, Cuba had won its independence, and the United States had won control of Puerto Rico, Guam, and the Philippine Islands. The Spanish-American War had

1850-1900

established the United States as a powerful nation. (*See* **Spanish-American War.**)

During the early 1900s, the United States continued to grow larger and stronger. Millions of immigrants arrived, mostly from Europe, and the population passed 100 million. These immigrants provided American industry with the large number of workers it needed. (*See* **immigration.**)

In 1914, World War I began in Europe. At first, the United States tried to stay out of the war. But German ships were attacking U.S. ships. In 1917, the U.S. joined Britain and France in fighting against Germany. The war ended on November 11, 1918, when Germany surrendered. (*See* **World War I.**)

During the 1920s, the U.S. enjoyed a time of fun and change. Women won the right to vote. They cut their hair short. "Flappers" wore short skirts. Everybody danced to a new kind of music called *jazz,* and people crowded the movie theaters. At home, they listened to radio programs. More Americans now lived in cities than on farms. Cities had skyscrapers and electric trolley cars.

The good times ended in 1929, when the Great Depression struck. At one point during this period, one-fourth of all workers in the United States were out of work. At the same time, there was a drought in the Great Plains. Crops failed. Farmers could not pay their debts and had to give up their farms. People moved to California and to the northern cities looking for work. Many people struggled to make a living or worried about losing their jobs. Some were so poor they could not buy food. Government leaders wondered what could be done to end the depression and to prevent another one from happening. (*See* **depression.**)

In 1932, Franklin D. Roosevelt was elected president. He promised the people a "New Deal." Congress passed programs that created public service jobs and prevented the loss of homes and farms. By the end of the 1930s, the economy was improving.

In 1939, World War II started in Europe. The war soon drew in nations in Asia and Africa. On December 7, 1941, Japan attacked U.S. forces in Hawaii. The United States declared war on Japan and on its allies—Germany and Italy. World War II continued another four and a half years. Japan was the last to surrender, after atomic bombs had been dropped on two of its cities. (*See* **World War II.**)

1900-1950

The United States and the Soviet Union both emerged from World War II as very powerful nations. During the war, the two nations were allies. But afterward, relations between them became strained. The Soviet Union forced its form of government—communism—on its neighboring nations. To prevent the spread of Soviet influence, the United States gave money and military aid to noncommunist nations.

In the early 1950s, the United States became involved in a war between communist North Korea and democratic South Korea. The United States was also involved in the dispute between Communists and non-Communists over control of South Vietnam. U.S. soldiers fought in Southeast Asia from the early 1960s until 1973. (*See* **Korean War** and **Vietnam War.**)

In the 1950s and 1960s, the U.S. economy was strong. Many businesses grew rapidly. During the 1960s, the U.S. space program sent astronauts into space and to the moon. (*See* **space exploration.**)

The 1960s were also a time of large political demonstrations. Black and white Americans protested the unequal treatment of black people in the United States. Their protests helped bring laws that made it illegal to treat people unfairly because of their color. In the late 1960s and early 1970s, many people also demonstrated against U.S. involvement in the Vietnam War.

In 1976, the United States celebrated its 200th birthday. The nation had a great deal to celebrate. Personal freedoms are still protected by law, and the nation's laws allow for change and for the correction of mistakes. There have sometimes been disagreements among the states, or between the federal government and the states. But the nation has found ways to work through the differences. The Constitution of the United States was 200 years old in 1987. It has proved a sound basis for solving differences and protecting the rights of American citizens.

Americans have contributed greatly to the world's scientific, medical, and technical knowledge. There have been many great American inventors, teachers, thinkers, artists, writers, and performers. The nation's natural resources and the hard work of its people have brought it a high standard of living. People from other countries look to the United States as a place where they will be safe and where they can speak freely.

1950-present

universe

The universe is made up of galaxies and space. It includes our sun and its solar system, all the other stars and heavenly objects, and all the light and energy they give off.

Many scientists think the universe began with a tremendous explosion. According to this "big bang theory," the explosion occurred about 18 billion years ago. It produced high temperatures and sent energy and matter flying outward in all directions. As the universe expanded from the force of the explosion, it cooled. Clouds of gases and dust began to collect and form into stars and other heavenly objects.

We do not know the size of the universe. Powerful starlike *quasars* are the most distant objects we can see. The light from a quasar takes about 12 million years to reach Earth. (*See* **quasar.**)

We know that the universe is still expanding, as the galaxies continually move away from each other. You can imagine the universe as a gigantic balloon. Inside the balloon is all the universe we can ever know. The universe may grow larger, but there is always an outside that we cannot know.

See also **galaxy.**

Unknown Soldier, Tomb of the

The Tomb of the Unknown Soldier is a memorial that honors U.S. soldiers killed in war who cannot be identified. It stands in Arlington National Cemetery, in Virginia.

After World War I (1914 to 1917), the United States decided to honor the many "unknown" soldiers killed in the war. The body of an unidentified U.S. soldier was taken from its grave in France and buried at Arlington on November 11, 1921—the third anniversary of the end of World War I.

Ten years later, a white marble monument was built over the grave. These words are carved on it: "Here rests in honored glory an American soldier known but to God." Soldiers guard the tomb day and night.

The Tomb of the Unknown Soldier in Arlington National Cemetery.

Today, three other unknown soldiers are buried at the memorial. These soldiers died in World War II (1939 to 1945), the Korean War (1950 to 1953), and the Vietnam War (1964 to 1973). The memorial is sometimes called the Tomb of the Unknowns.

uranium

Uranium is a metal used as a fuel in nuclear reactors and in some nuclear bombs. Of all the elements found in nature, uranium has the highest *atomic number*—92. It also has the greatest *atomic mass*—238. The atomic number is the number of protons in the *nucleus*—center—of an atom. The atomic mass is the number of protons and neutrons in the nucleus. (*See* **element.**)

Uranium is *radioactive*—it sends out high-energy particles and rays. Radioactive elements break down into other elements. Uranium by itself is not very radioactive, but the elements it changes into are very radioactive. These include polonium, radium, and radon. (*See* **radioactivity** and **radium.**)

Uranium's high atomic mass makes it unstable. Most uranium is a form called *uranium-238*. It has 92 protons and 146 neutrons. If one more neutron is added, the whole atom sometimes breaks apart into the atoms of other elements. The atomic numbers of the new atoms will add up to 92. The process is called *nuclear fission*.

In a nuclear reactor, materials that absorb neutrons easily—such as carbon or ordinary water—keep the neutrons at the right level. The goal is to keep the fission going and producing energy, but at the same time to make sure there are not enough neutrons to cause an explosion. If the controls fail, the additional neutrons produce more fission, which produces more neutrons. Finally, uncontrolled fission will result in an explosion.

See also **nuclear power** and **nuclear weapon.**

Uranus

Uranus is the seventh planet out from the sun in our solar system. Its orbit keeps it about 2.9 billion kilometers (1.8 billion miles) from the sun.

Uranus is the third-largest planet. Its diameter is 51,200 kilometers (32,000 miles). The planet is a big ball of very cold gases, mostly hydrogen and helium. Astronomers think it has a solid, rocky core. Uranus has at least 15 moons and a set of faint rings around its equator.

Perhaps the strangest feature of Uranus is how it *rotates*—spins. All planets rotate as they travel around the sun. This creates

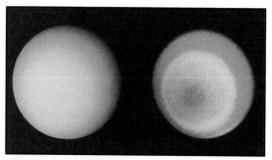

Uranus from *Voyager 2*—in natural color and in bright artificial colors.

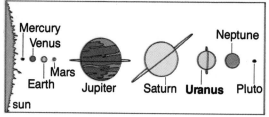

night and day. For some reason, Uranus lies on its side and rolls like a ball. The other planets spin like tops. Uranus's trip around the sun takes 84 Earth years. Because of the way Uranus rotates, daytime and summer last the same amount of time, 42 Earth years. Nighttime and winter likewise last 42 years. Yet Uranus rotates on its axis once in a little less than 17 hours.

Uranus was discovered in 1781 by Sir William Herschel. The planet is so far away from Earth that it can barely be seen through a telescope. Astronomers had little information about Uranus until 1986. Then the U.S. spaceprobe *Voyager 2* passed by it. *Voyager 2* sent back much information and closeup pictures of the planet.

Uruguay, *see* South America

Utah

Capital: Salt Lake City
Area: 84,899 square miles (219,888 square kilometers) (11th-largest state)
Population (1980): 1,461,037 (1985): about 1,645,000 (35th-largest state)
Became a state: January 4, 1896 (45th state)

Utah is a state located in the western United States. Utah is bordered on the north by Wyoming and Idaho, on the east by Colorado, on the west by Nevada, and on the south by Arizona.

Land Utah's highest point is Kings Peak, in the Uinta Range of the Rocky Mountains. Kings Peak is 13,528 feet (4,123 meters) above sea level. (*See* **Rocky Mountains.**)

Southeastern Utah is a land of plateaus. In places, they look like giant steps along the Colorado River. There are huge, colorful cliffs 2,000 feet (610 meters) high. The western part of Utah consists of short mountain ranges separated by wide, flat valleys.

During the Ice Age, an enormous body of water called Lake Bonneville stretched across parts of Utah. When most of this lake dried up, Great Salt Lake formed. Its waters are up to seven times saltier than seawater. (*See* **Great Salt Lake.**)

Summers are warm in Utah, and winters are cold. The state is dry, except in the Rocky Mountains. Sometimes, the snow is more than 100 inches (2,538 millimeters) deep in the high mountain valleys.

Nature has created fascinating landscapes in Utah. Rivers have cut deep gorges and canyons. Wind has shaped rocks into natural bridges. The largest natural bridge in the world is in southern Utah. Many fossils of prehistoric animals are preserved at Dinosaur National Monument, which Utah shares with neighboring Colorado.

Lake Powell is part of the Glen Canyon National Recreation Area in southern Utah.

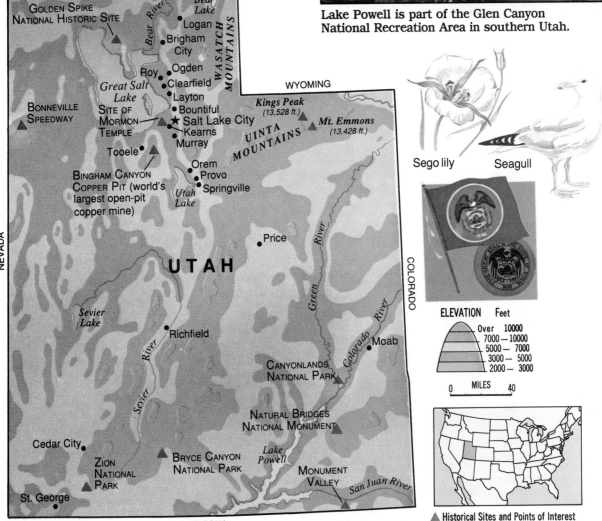

Sego lily   Seagull

ELEVATION   Feet

Over 10000
7000 — 10000
5000 — 7000
3000 — 5000
2000 — 3000

0   MILES   40

▲ Historical Sites and Points of Interest

Utah is a leading producer of copper, gold, silver, and lead. It also has some oil. The world's largest deposit of oil shale lies beneath the surface of Utah, Colorado, and Wyoming.

The world's richest copper mine is in Bingham Canyon, Utah. This gigantic open pit supplies more than one-fifth of all the copper mined in the United States.

Many parts of Utah are used for raising sheep, cattle, and other *livestock*—farm animals. Farmlands must be irrigated. Utah's chief crops are apricots, cherries, sugar beets, and potatoes.

History Hundreds of years ago, Anasazi Indians built homes in the cliffs of southeastern Utah. Ute, Shoshone, and Paiute Indians were living in Utah when European explorers arrived in the 1700s. Navaho Indians first came to the area in the 1860s.

The Spanish explored Utah during the late 1700s. The region became part of Mexico in 1821. There were no permanent settlements in Utah until 1847, when the first group of Mormons arrived.

Mormons are members of the Church of Jesus Christ of the Latter-Day Saints. The church was organized in New York State in 1830. The Mormons were often made to suffer for their beliefs. They traveled west looking for a place where they could live in peace. They tried Ohio, Missouri, Illinois, and Nebraska before going to Utah. There, they founded Salt Lake City and many other communities. Using new irrigation methods, they grew wheat, corn, and other crops.

In 1848, the United States defeated Mexico in the Mexican War. As a result, the United States received a large area of Mexican land that included Utah. In 1850, the U.S. Congress created the Utah Territory. The Mormon leader Brigham Young was chosen as the territory's first governor. The Mormons called their territory *Deseret.* This word, taken from Mormon scriptures, means "honeybee." The name stood for hard work.

For many years, the federal government refused to grant statehood to Utah. This was mainly because of the Mormons' acceptance of *polygamy.* This is the practice of allowing a man to be married to more than one woman at a time. The Mormons outlawed polygamy in 1890, and Utah became a state in 1896.

In 1861, telegraph lines from Washington, D.C., and San Francisco were joined at Salt Lake City, creating the nation's first coast-to-coast telegraph service. The country's first transcontinental railroad was also completed in Utah, at Promontory in 1869.

People Almost three-fourths of the people of Utah are Mormons. Most of the population is clustered in a 150-mile (242-kilometer) strip of fertile land in the Wasatch Range, a branch of the Rockies in north-central Utah. The largest cluster is in and around the state capital, Salt Lake City.

Salt Lake City is an important commercial, industrial, and transportation center. It is also headquarters of the Mormon church. Among the city's famous buildings are the Mormon temple, tabernacle, assembly hall, and museum, all in Temple Square.

For years, most people in Utah worked in agriculture or mining. During the 1900s, manufacturing and tourism became the main economic activities. Utah produces transportation equipment, food, machinery, metal products, and electrical equipment. It is also important in the aerospace industry.

See also **Mormons** and **Young, Brigham.**

Rock carvings made by Indians over many years at Indian Creek, Utah.